BestMasters

Springer awards "BestMasters" to the best master's theses which have been completed at renowned universities in Germany, Austria, and Switzerland.
The studies received highest marks and were recommended for publication by supervisors. They address current issues from various fields of research in natural sciences, psychology, technology, and economics.
The series addresses practitioners as well as scientists and, in particular, offers guidance for early stage researchers.

Kathleen Kürschner

Immigration and Housing Rents

Evidence from German Reunification

Springer Gabler

Kathleen Kürschner
Magdeburg, Germany

BestMasters
ISBN 978-3-658-12060-3 ISBN 978-3-658-12061-0 (eBook)
DOI 10.1007/978-3-658-12061-0

Library of Congress Control Number: 2015954814

Springer Gabler

Printed on acid-free paper

Springer Gabler is a brand of Springer Fachmedien Wiesbaden
Springer Fachmedien Wiesbaden is part of Springer Science+Business Media
(www.springer.com)

Preface

The fall of the Berlin Wall on 9th November 1989 sparked a mass exodus of East Germans to West Germany. This work exploits the natural experiment provided by the unexpected disintegration of socialist East Germany to study the impact of the mass immigration of East Germans on housing rents in West German metropolitan areas. Using a spatial correlation approach, annual district-level migration data for 1991 and 1992 and unique rental price indicators from Germany's major regional property market information system, we find strong evidence for a positive and sizeable effect of immigration on rental prices of residential housing. A one percent population increase due to immigration is associated with an approximate increase in minimum and average category rents by 4.8 and 3.3 percent, respectively. Additional explorations that employ an IV approach based on various exogenous origin-region push factors related to the deteriorating economic conditions in East Germany yield estimates of even larger magnitude. These results suggest that immigration has important economic effects outside the labour market, traditionally the prime domain of economic enquiries into the consequences of immigration. Our findings cast doubt on the appropriateness of this bias in focus.

Kathleen Kürschner (M.Sc.)
Magdeburg, September 2015

Contents

List of Figures

List of Tables

List of Abbreviations

2SLS	-	Two-Stage Least Squares
BTE	-	Berufstaetigenerhebung (workforce census)
COMECON	-	Council for Mutual Economic Assistance
CPI	-	Consumer Price Index
D-Mark	-	Deutschemark (former currency of the Federal Republic of Germany)
EOD	-	Employment Office District
FRG	-	Federal Republic of Germany
GDR	-	German Democratic Republic
IV	-	Instrumental Variable
LPG	-	Landwirtschaftliche Produktionsgenossenschaft (agricultural cooperative)
MSA	-	Metropolitan Statistical Area
OECD	-	Organisation for Economic Co- operation and Development
OEEC	-	Organisation for European Economic Co-operation
OLS	-	Ordinary Least Squares
P&P	-	Push and Pull (factors)
PPP	-	Purchasing Power Parity
RIWIS	-	RIWIS bulwiengesa AG

SEMU	-	Social Economic and Monetary Union
UK	-	United Kingdom
U.S.	-	United States of America
WWII	-	The Second World War
ZER	-	Zentrales Einwohnerregister Berlin-Biesdorf

List of Symbols

Δ	-	First-difference (long-difference)
β_0	-	Main regression model constant
$\beta_1 \ldots \beta_4$	-	Main regression model coefficients
γ_0	-	Preliminary regression model constant
$\boldsymbol{\gamma_1}$	-	Vector of preliminary regression model coefficients
$\varepsilon_{j,1990-92}$	-	Idiosyncratic error term
μ_j	-	Set of market type dummies
ρ_j	-	Set of state dummies
σ^2	-	Variance
φ_j	-	Zonal border area dummy (metropolitan destination)
ω_i	-	Zonal border area dummy (origin)
c	-	Rental category
$D_{i,j}$	-	Distance
H_0	-	Null hypothesis
i	-	Origin area (migrant sending area)
j	-	Metropolitan area (migrant recipient area)
k	-	Industrial sector
$area_i$	-	Area in square kilometre

$arr_{j,1990}$	-	Annual guest arrivals (check-in at local hospitality providers)
$impact_{k,i}$	-	Shock impact
$m_{i,j,1991-92}$	-	Observed migration (detailed)
$\widehat{m}_{i,j,1991-92}$	-	Predicted migration (detailed)
$m_{j,1991-92}$	-	Immigration divided by initial population (main explanatory variable)
$pop_{j,1990}$	-	(initial) population
$production\ decline_k$	-	Export industry induced production decline in sector *k*
$rent_{j,c,1990-92}$	-	Rental outcomes (endogenous variables)
$sector\ share_{k,i}$	-	Local employment concentration in sector *k*
$spec$	-	Specification of preliminary regression model
$u_{j,1990}$	-	Unemployment rate (annual average)
$v_{i,j,1991-92}$	-	Error term (preliminary regression)
$working\ pop_{i,1990}$	-	(initial) working population
$\hat{z}_{i,j,1991-92}$	-	Instrumental variable (detailed)
$\hat{z}_{j,1991-92}$	-	Instrumental variable (cumulated)

1 Introduction

The phenomenon *migration* traces back to the dawn of mankind. Indeed, migrants have been induced to relocate by various intrinsic as well as extrinsic motives ever since. Thence, the complexity of these so called *push and pull factors (P&P)*, the driving forces that shape individuals' decision to migrate, brought about highly diversified and ever changing migrant streams until present.[1]

Connotatively, historical events played a pivotal role in the facilitation of migrant stocks and flows in terms of volume and pattern. Factually, the earliest notable labour market induced movements have been expressed in huge waves of forced migration in the mode of slavery trade throughout the 15th and 16th century. Similarly, indentured labour flows accounted for a large proportion of migrants during the 19th century, which was furthermore accompanied by voluntary mass emigration from European countries to traditional migrant destinations, particularly the *United States of America (U.S.)*. The mass movements reached their peak period by the beginning of the 20th century, triggered by the vast industrialisation advancements throughout preceding decades. Voluntary migration came essentially to a halt during the *Second World War (WWII)*, which was followed by a mass displacement of roughly eight million expelled Germans from Eastern Europe to West Germany.[2]

Moreover, aspects associated with globalisation, such as reductions in travel cost as well as declining barriers to entry and exit that went hand in hand with the establishment of international affiliations and trade

1 See Bodvarsson, Ö. B. and H. Van den Berg (2009), pp. 7-11.
2 See loc. cit., pp. 12-13.

agreements, played an important role in the revival of international migration over the past five to six decades.[3] Consequently, the scope and persistency of the migration phenomenon attracted a vast number of scholars to study its many facets, contributing to a large strand of literature on the topic. Prevailingly, early research efforts gave rise to a controversial debate on potential positive and negative effects of migration for both sending and recipient areas in perspective. In particular, the study of the labour market impact and associated consequences for natives gained most attention in this debate. Notwithstanding, the corresponding results generally lack consistency and are lower in magnitude than initially expected.[4] Thence, recent research contributions have pointed towards the utilisation of a more holistic view of migrants' impact on host economies.[5] The investigative focus has lately shifted to the study of local price dynamics of traded and non-traded goods and services in response to immigration. In this regard, the migration impact on residential property markets of destination economies is currently a relatively unexplored area of expertise.[6]

In addition, research endeavours over the past two decades have involved the study of yet another eminent historical event that reshaped international migration: The collapse of the communist era in numerous Eurasian countries triggered a dramatic migration wave to Western Europe from 1990 onwards.[7] This very recent historical episode, associated with the fall of the Berlin Wall, elucidated the mass migration of Eastern Germans to West Germany from 1989 onwards. Today, more than 25 years after German reunification, it prevails that this regime

3 See Stalker, P. (2000), p. 7.
4 See Friedberg, R. M. and J. Hunt (1995), pp. 30-35.
5 See Massey, D. S. et al. (1993), p. 432.
6 See Saiz, A. (2007); Gonzales, L. and F. Ortega (2013), among others.
7 See Bodvarsson, Ö. B. and H. Van den Berg (2009), p. 13.

change was inherently connected to the migration potential that built up behind the iron curtain over several decades of suppression.[8] The pioneering efforts of those willing to emigrate from the *German Democratic Republic (GDR)* triggered a dramatic series of events that eluded power of the communist government and initiated an enduring social and economic transition process that may be considered 'work in progress' ever since.

Consequently, the purpose of this thesis is to investigate the impact of immigration on property prices in metropolitan West Germany in the wake of German reunification. In this respect, inner German migrant streams throughout 1991 and 1992 will be focused on. The specified time period has been chosen to exploit the natural experiment character of this setting, which is a supportive tool to circumvent attenuation bias in conducting empirical research.[9] In addition, the study aims to develop a profound instrumentation technique based on the unique features of this historical episode. The findings of the underlying analysis are based on secondary and empirical research. The thesis proceeds as follows: An overview of the existing literature on the topic will be provided in Chapter 2, alongside a brief representation of the historical setting which builds the foundation for the ensuing investigation. The methodological approach to encounter the topic will be depicted in Chapter 3. Departing from an introduction of the underlying empirical model, the explored data sources are presented in conjunction with an elaboration of relevant time trends, surrounding the period studied. Chapter 4 serves to quantify and discuss the results of the empirical analysis. The study will be concluded in Chapter 5.

---

8 See Schumann, K. F. (1996), pp. 33-35.

9 See Friedberg, R. M. and J. Hunt (1995), pp. 36-37.

2 Background

The purpose of this chapter is to establish the fundamental concepts upon which the proceeding study rests. To accomplish that, a review of the existing literature, associated with the analysis of migration and housing prices, is depicted in Section 2.1. Furthermore, Section 2.2 serves to provide a brief summary of the historical events that shaped German reunification and motivated the exploitation of this natural experiment in the underlying thesis.

2.1 Related Literature

The nature of *the migration phenomenon* is characterised by its universal presence across the globe and persistency over time, which attracted a vast number of scholars to contribute to a large strand of literature on the topic. Due to the complexity of the factors and processes that drive migration and the associated consequences thereof, the related literature may be subdivided into two major categories: The first branch relates to theories that evolved from the analysis of the *determinants of migration*. In particular, this category focuses on the structure of the P&P factors that trigger migration and result in the observable aggregate migrant streams *per se*.[10] In addition, a sub-group of this branch relates to the degree at which migrants are selected. That is, the composition of the migrant streams in terms of individuals' characteristics, such as, migrants' state of education, professional qualifications and the like. However, both subgroups are closely related to each other and in a way condensed in the theory underlying the Borjas model of *migrant*

10 See Bodvarsson, Ö. B. and H. Van den Berg (2009), pp. 7-9, among others.

selection,[11] which is an adaptation of A. D. Roy's fundamental "[...] thoughts on the distribution of earnings"[12] in 1951. Nevertheless, specifically the consideration of migrants' educational stance induced a fiery debate, in the early 1960s and '70s, on the existence of a *brain drain* related to emigration of the highly skilled; which moreover, experienced a revival in the 1990s.[13] Accordingly, the consideration of related consequences for host and home countries establishes one of the many linkages to the second branch of literature, which is dedicated to the *impact of migration* on sending and recipient areas. It prevails, that the empirical literature of this branch is intensely slanted towards the labour market impact of migration. Although interesting from a political point of view, the results of related studies are somewhat puzzling, since the suggested immigration impacts on destination labour market outcomes are in most instances unexpectedly small in magnitude or inconclusive.[14]

In order to address this issue, recent research endeavours pointed toward the necessity to incorporate a larger variety of factors when analysing the impact of immigration on the well-being of natives. The reasoning behind the construction of more holistic migration models stems from a consideration of potential explanations for the controversial results that were drawn from existing labour market studies: First of all, the influx of migrants to a destination area may increase competition on the local labour market; thereby, inducing an outflow of natives thereof. Such spill-over effects lead to labour market equalisation on the grounds of

11 See Borjas, G. J. (1987), pp. 532-537.
12 Roy, A. D. (1951), p. 135.
13 See Grubel, H. and A. Scott (1966); Carrington, W. J. and E. Detragiache (1998), among others.
14 See Friedberg, R. M. and J. Hunt (1995), pp. 30-35; Pischke, J. S. and J. Velling (1997), p. 594.

internal migration to areas that arc characterised by more favourable labour market conditions. Hence, the increase in competition for jobs due to the arrival of migrants may be relatively short-lived and difficult to observe, since wages arguably do not adjust instantaneously to changes in the labour supply.[15]

Second, the workforce composition of destination areas is altered depending on immigrants' characteristics. Precisely, if migrants are close substitutes to natives, a change in the relative wage structure among different skill groups, and thus, production cost likely prevails. Moreover, the arrival of migrants with primarily complementing skill sets would likely yield an increase in productivity, hence, reducing production cost and additionally, opening up an alleyway for local economic growth prospects. Altogether, immigration may exhibit an upward or downward pressure on prices due to changes in the local labour force composition. However, the degree to which this effect is translated into actual price changes largely depends on the degree at which the respective products and services are traded in the economy. Commonly, the non-traded goods sector passes production-cost-induced price changes on to their customers. At the same time, changes in the demand structure for those goods, due to immigration, will likewise be replicated in price changes. Hence, inferring the third explanation of the ambiguous labour market impact of migration: Migrants' arrival increases demand for local consumption goods, thence, stimulating local economic activity.[16]

Indeed, how immigrant demand affects destination economies is an important issue that allows to draw a more concise picture of the factors

[15] See Card, D. (1990), pp. 255-256.
[16] See Kalantaryan, S. (2013), p. 2.

driving migration as well as the associated consequences for the local economy and natives' welfare. Thus, recent studies have been directed at an examination of the migration impact on prices of goods and services in destination economies. For instance, in a first study on the pricing dynamics of non-traded goods across U.S. cities, in response to immigration of the low-skilled, a decreasing impact on prices of migrant intensive services has been suggested. That is, a one percent increase in the low-skilled immigrant share of an average U.S. city's labour force is claimed to decrease the price of services that are predominantly offered by this group, such as gardening and housekeeping, by 0.2 percent. Accordingly, it is argued that natives benefitted from immigration in the form of a reduction in the cost of living component of migrant intensive services. Nevertheless, the suggested benefits are accompanied by a reallocation of wealth, through alterations in *purchasing power parity (PPP)* across different skill groups. Precisely, the respective study exploits *consumer price index (CPI)* data from 1980 to 2000, moreover identifying an increase in the PP of the highly skilled by, on average, 0.32 percent; while the PP of high school drop outs and low skilled Hispanic inhabitants has been reduced by up to one and 4.2 percent, respectively.[17]

The above findings have been further supported by a similar study on the price impact of immigration in the *United Kingdom (UK)* between 1995 and 2006. Equally employing regional CPI data on roughly 300 surveyed items, the analysis has been extended to the tradeable goods sector. Although similarly small in magnitude to the outcomes for the U.S., a dual effect across sectors prevails: A predominantly high concentration of low-skilled migrants in the service sector, showed a price reducing

---

[17] See, Cortes, P. (2008), pp. 413-414.

effect through the associated increase in labour supply. That is, a one percentage point increase in the local immigrant share, led to a 0.2 percent decrease in the remuneration of services. On the contrary, the demand increase in low-value groceries, which is arguably linked to the prevalent increase in the UK migrant stock of the latter group over the past decades, had driven prices up in this market segment. Taking both effects into consideration, it is once again pointed towards a redistribution of welfare away from the native low-level income group, since particularly the mid to upper-level earners are suggested to benefit from the consumption of non-tradeable services, which experienced a price decline. At the same time, the PP of the relatively poor has been decreased through rising prices of essential low-value groceries.[18]

Contrarily, a further related study on the mass arrival of former Soviet Union migrants to Israel during the 1990s has shown opposing results. However, the surveyed sample differs in that the price dynamics of 915 store-level CPI products are explored, hence, excluding the service sector. Accordingly, controlling for native population size as well as city and month effects provided evidence for a negative relationship between immigration and prices: It is claimed that a one percentage point increase in a destination's immigrant share decreased prices by, on average, 0.5 percentage points. Nevertheless, the estimated effect of this very large and unexpected migrant inflow, equal to roughly four percent of the initial population, is suggested to be largely attributable to differences in demand characteristics of migrants and natives. On the grounds that emigrants' demand was more price elastic and combined with extensive price comparison efforts, likely motivated by relatively low search costs, it is argued that local grocery owners were induced to lower prices in

---

[18] See Frattini, T. (2008), pp. 1-3.

order to attract the newly arrived consumers to extend their customer base.[19]

Altogether, the analyses of immigrants' influence on pricing dynamics have shown that the effects differ largely among traded and non-traded goods and services. In particular, the consideration of the non-traded goods sector attracted further attention, which has been expressed in research endeavours on migrants' impact on housing price dynamics. This topic is of particular interest as it typifies a special case of non-tradeable goods in destination economies that represents a particularly large fraction of natives' living cost expenses. Indeed, this relatively unexplored field of research attracted first attention in the 1980s. Although, the initial studies were mostly of descriptive nature, a strong relationship between immigration and property prices had been suggested, which provided a profound fundament for subsequent empirical research endeavours.[20] Motivated by Card's analysis of the Mariel Boatlift in 1990, which explores the labour market impact of migration in a natural experiment setting, [21] Susin and Saiz were the first to conduct empirical analyses of associated housing market impacts.[22] The sudden mass arrival of approximately 125,000 Cuban immigrants increased Miami's tenant population by an additional nine percent, which was intuitively bound to have an effect on wages and rental prices. However, the local labour market apparently absorbed the additional supply of low-skilled labour very well, affecting wages only moderately.[23] However, the opposite was observed for the development

19 See Lach, S. (2007), pp. 548-551.

20 See Muller, T. and T. J. Espenshade (1985); Ley, D. and J. Tuchener (2001), among others.

21 See Card, D. (1990), p. 245.

22 See Susin, S. (2001) and Saiz, A. (2003).

23 See Card, D. (1990), pp. 256-257.

of rental prices: the application of a difference in differences approach to this historical event produced empirical evidence of a rental price increase, which exceeded the ones of the respective control groups by eight to eleven percent. This finding is substantial in magnitude, particularly in the light of the fact that wages remained relatively stable throughout the surveyed time period of 1979 to 1982. In addition, the results allow a comparison of the impact on different rental categories, revealing that particularly low level income households, which rely on the lower bound rentals, have been affected by the letting price rise. Contrary to that, prices among the upper level categories have been characterised by a relative decline, providing once more evidence for the presence of redistributive effects, from the relatively poor to the relatively rich. However, the results do not suffice for general conclusions to be drawn, due to the high specificity of the observed location and time frame.[24]

An opposing view to this argument emerged from a more generalised consideration of the joint income and rental price development in response to migrant inflows. The related study on the rent to income ratio employs decennial data, from 1980 to 2000, on the 91 largest *metropolitan statistical areas (MSA)* in the U.S. The findings suggest no significant change in the average rent to income ratio, that is, the so called *rental burden* on natives. Moreover, it is proposed that there is no disproportionate impact on natives, who are more likely to compete for housing with immigrants. Much of this counterfactual outcome has been attributed to the capacity of housing markets to adjust fairly well over the longer run, since the survey is based on decennial changes.[25] Furthermore, in an attempt to conduct a first general equilibrium

---

24 See Saiz, A. (2003), p. 518.
25 See Greulich, E. et al. (2004), pp. 183-185.

approach employing census data over three decades from 1970 to 2000 in combination with American Community Survey data for 2005, a causal relationship between immigration and housing rents across states and metropolitan areas has been suggested. In addition, evidence for differential impacts on natives with different schooling attainment has been provided, contradicting the latter study. The respective scholars argue that immigration had a significantly positive impact on rents of the highly and less educated. At the same time, the highly educated benefitted from increasing wages due to complementarities in production, while the less educated faced small but negative wage effects. Notably, the proposition that particularly the rental outcomes of the highly skilled were highly sensitive to immigration is somewhat outstanding among this branch of literature.[26]

In addition, a separate investigation of the immigration impact on average wages by David Card in 2007 has shown that the impact on wages among major U.S. cities is positive,[27] and moreover, of similar magnitude to the analogously observed average increase in rental prices by Albert Saiz in 2007.[28] In spite of the provided insight that the burden of living expenses remained approximately constant on average, the dispersion of the wage gap among natives in different skill-groups has arguably increased, lending further support to the welfare redistribution argument, discussed above. Thence, the study further points towards the necessity to consider the multilevel impact of immigration on the well-being of natives, beyond the sheer consideration of labour market

---

26 See Ottaviano, G. I.P. and G. Peri (2007), pp. 1-3.
27 See Card, D. (2007), p. 3.
28 See Saiz, A. (2007), p. 346.

effects. This is particularly important considering the formulation of appropriate immigration policy responses.[29]

Prevailingly, the seminal contributions to this relatively new strand of literature have been largely involved with analyses of the U.S. housing market and other traditional migrant destinations, which have featured a large foreign born composition of the population throughout history. It is thence surprising, that the results across those destination areas differ largely. For instance, the pioneering study on rental price dynamics in U.S.-MSAs between 1985 and 1998 by Albert Saiz in 2007, suggests that a one percent increase in the surveyed cities' population is associated with a one percent increase in average rents, which essentially provided a baseline result for subsequent studies and the present thesis. This result moreover translates into an income reducing effect that is an order of magnitude larger than comparable wage reductions, associated with a one percent increase in the relative share of a specific skill group among the labour force, due to immigration.[30] In addition, in a recent research contribution on the Canadian housing market, it is argued that there was a significant positive, yet restrained, impact of immigration on rents.[31]

In contrast, a study of local housing market dynamics in New Zealand, between 1986 and 2006, does neither provide empirical evidence for a positive causal effect of foreign-born immigration on local property prices nor rents. It is merely argued that an overall population increase by one percent is associated with a rental price increase of 0.2 to 0.5 percent. However, since there is no obvious link between the local

---

29 See Card, D. (2007), pp. 31-33.
30 See Saiz, A. (2007), pp. 363-364.
31 See Akbari, A. H. and Y. Aydede (2012), p. 1645.

housing price increases and changes in the share of the foreign born population, the driving forces are likely more complex. Interestingly, return migration is suggested to exhibit an upward pressure on property prices in the given setting: A one percent population increase due to higher return migration of natives yields a six to nine percent increase in local housing prices. In an extension to the neighbourhood level, the outcomes are supportive of the main result considering general population growth, yet boroughs that are characterised by larger foreign-born inflows featured relatively lower property price growth than surrounding areas. Nevertheless, the respective outcomes are not robust over time.[32]

Departing from the traditional immigrant recipient countries, more recent studies have explored the impact of immigration on housing markets in European countries. Precisely, a seminal research contribution focused on the immigration wave to Spain, between 2000 and 2010, which was accompanied by a boom in regional housing prices. The respective scholars find that immigration accounted for approximately 25 percent of the observed housing price increase during the surveyed decade as well as 50 percent of the construction activity. The empirical evidence suggests that an average 1.5 percent annual increase in the working population due to immigration induced a rental price rise of roughly two percent and increased construction activity by 1.2 to 1.5 percent.[33]

Moreover, a contemporary study of the Italian housing market focuses on the recently observed immigration phenomenon to the country, exploring data from 1996 to 2007. In this primary analysis of the migration impact on Italian rents, evidence for a positive, yet declining

32 See Stillman, S. and D. C. Maré (2008), pp. 27-28.
33 See Gonzales, L. and F. Ortega (2013), pp. 37-39.

price growth has been suggested: A ten percent increase in the local foreign-born population is associated with a 0.6 percent increase in average property prices. In addition, the corresponding results of the related instrumental variable estimation suggest a significant impact of slightly larger magnitude, which is in line with previous studies. Nonetheless, the outcomes for the Italian property market are comparably small in magnitude and of non-linear form. That is, the growth rate of the local foreign-born share features a threshold at roughly three percent, likewise five to six percent in the instrumental variable approach, after which the speed of housing price appreciation declined.[34]

Remarkably, many of the presented housing market analyses have considered time periods that were characterised by particularly large migrant inflows, which moreover, coincided with the build-up and burst of the construction and housing bubble that was associated with the onset of the worst global economic crisis since WWII.[35] Therefore, a study on the Swiss property market has been conducted with the aim to provide further evidence for the existence of the elaborated immigration impact on property price dynamics, in the presence of fundamentally low house price inflation. The Swiss property market is well suited for this research endeavour, as it features rental controls on a nationwide basis, low occupancy turnover- as well as comparably low homeownership rates. In addition, immigration to the country throughout the surveyed period from 2001 to 2006 has been moderate, accounting for an approximate annual inflow worth 0.3 percent of the native population. The related study confirms the existence of a significant positive causal effect of immigration on housing prices in the presence of modest immigration

34 See Kalantaryan, S. (2013), pp. 21-22.
35 See Papademetriou, D. G. et al. (2010), p. 4.

and low inflation: An increase in the local population by one percent due to immigration is associated with a 2.7 percent increase in prices of single-family dwellings.[36]

Altogether, the presented studies indicate that the presence of an immigration impact on housing markets is a global phenomenon. Nevertheless, this area of expertise is still relatively unexplored and there has been no general consensus on the magnitude and/or direction of the proposed effect. Consequently, the present thesis attempts to follow the approach of the presented contributions to this emerging field of interest, applying a spatial correlation analysis to West German metropolitan property markets. The time period studied is very specific from a historical point of view and focuses on a relatively limited time frame, which is characterised by mass immigration of East Germans, shortly after the fall of the Berlin Wall. However, the results, depicted in Chapter 4, show a similar pattern to the pendants from the study of the Mariel Boatlift,[37] suggesting that the degree to which migration is unpredictable or unexpected may play an important role in this consideration. Both of the considered natural experiments most obviously incorporated a large degree of unpredictability, as they allow to study the response of housing markets to shifts in demand, caused by an unexpected mass inflow of migrants, triggered by abrupt political regime changes in their home countries.

Accordingly, the underlying investigation also touches upon a third complex branch of migration literature that emerged in the wake of German reunification, a detailed elaboration of which is, however, beyond the scope of this thesis. Altogether, it may be summarised that

---

36 See Degen, K. and A. M. Fischer (2010), pp. 1-4.

37 See Saiz, A. (2003), p. 518.

numerous scholars have been attracted to apply the previously established theories on the *determinants and impacts of migration* to this historical event, in order to exploit its natural experiment character. However, turning back to the multifaceted studies on labour market impacts, related contributions by Pischke and Velling in 1997, and likewise Douglas Frank in 2009, yield moreover outcomes that negate a significant impact on natives' employment outcomes. Specifically, Frank surveys local labour market data between 1990 and 1997, suggesting that there was neither a significant impact on natives' wages nor any redistributive effects among differing groups in terms of educational attainment, occupational status or gender. In line with the literature on the price impact, surveyed above, he argues that workers who engaged in the production of non-traded goods and services were made, if at all, relatively worse of.[38]

The study by Douglas Frank is, from a technical point of view, of particular interest to the underlying investigation. In order to address potential endogeneity concerns regarding migrants' relocation patterns, he constructs instruments on the basis of origin area characteristics that are presumably exogenous to the labour market outcomes in the surveyed destination areas. More specifically, he utilises available data on labour market characteristics in 25 East German *employment office districts (EOD)* and interacts the respective pushing forces with four distance categories to potential destinations in the West, in order to describe how migrants are distributed across the recipient areas. In order to accomplish that, he runs a separate regression of individually observed migrant streams on various labour market indicators to predict exogenous migration. This pertinent approach differs in several ways

38 See Pischke, J. S. and J. Velling (1997), p. 594; Frank, D. (2009), p. 3.

from the ones typically applied in the discussed housing market studies: First, the entire set of recent contributions utilises the presence of migrant networks to describe the exogenous variation in migrants' location choices. An exception is the exploitation of an additional instrument, based on gateways. That is, the assessment of the relative accessibility of local areas by air-, sea- or motorways, which typically varies across origin as well as destination regions, dependent on established infrastructures.[39] Second, none of the related studies conduct an auxiliary regression analysis to predict emigration from surveyed origin areas, apart from Albert Saiz in 2007.[40]

The present investigation adapts this instrumentation approach in order to most accurately predict exogenous immigration to the surveyed West German metropolitan areas. However, the indicators generated to account for the pushing forces differ from the ones used by Douglas Frank, who applies unemployment rates and indicators for the quality of available jobs.[41] In contrast, the present study resorts to a conceptual theory of international trade, which serves to explain one of the many factors that led to deteriorating economic conditions in East Germany in the aftermath of reunification. Thence, the following section is dedicated to develop a brief overview of the associated historical background, as a basis for the proceeding analysis.

39 See Gonzales, L. and F. Ortega (2013), pp. 43-44.
40 See Saiz, A. (2007), pp. 357-358.
41 See Frank, D. (2009), pp. 22-23.

2.2 Historical Background

Following the German defeat in WWII, the country had been split among the allied forces into four occupation zones. In a prompt reaction to the differentiate prosecution strategies of the Soviets, the establishment of the former Soviet occupation zone was immediately accompanied by an initial wave of refugees thereof. Indeed, this development transformed into a persistent outflow of political refugees that lasted beyond the foundation of the GDR on 7th October 1949.[42]

The implementation of centrally planned economic structures in this newly founded republic was characterised by expropriations and the introduction of economy wide production plans, initially covering a two year period and five years thereafter. Apart from the fact that the GDR was obliged to pay the largest reparations among all defeated combatants of WWII, its precarious establishment was rapidly followed by several economic challenges as well as political repressions, which drove up citizens' flight from the republic that culminated in the construction of the Berlin Wall on 13th August in 1961. The political motivation of this extraordinary measure rested upon the prevalent human capital flight from the GDR. On the one hand, the massive outflow of the young and highly skilled posed further challenges to the future economic development that would likely translate into a continued malfunctioning of the centrally planned economy. On the other hand, it was tantamount to the benefit of the *Federal Republic of Germany (FRG)*. In spite of the fact that this radical measure lend some degree of protection to those in power and essentially put a halt to the flight from the republic, it did not help to overcome the profound economic problems of the GDR.[43]

42 See Schumann, K. F. (1996), pp. 16-17.
43 See Steiner, A. (2013), pp. 17-27.

Conversely, the associated political repressions induced an enormous accumulation of migration potential, over more than 25 years, which was released with the fall of the Berlin Wall on 9th November 1989. In fact, towards the end of the 1980s, the joint sentiment of the population regarding dissatisfaction with the eroded political apparatus, enduring economic hardship and suppressed freedom, found its expression in the peaceful mass protests throughout the summer and fall of 1989. At the same time, a loosening of the established travel restrictions triggered a resubmission wave of formerly rejected emigration and travel applications, which escalated in the occupation of German embassies in Hungary and the former CSSR as well as a wave of illegal mass emigration via those gateway countries. This dramatic series of events ultimately led to the regime collapse, which was followed by the reunification of the two German countries.[44]

It prevails, that much of this rapid transformation is attributable to the pioneering efforts and sacrifices of the former East German political refugees and protesters. Notwithstanding, emigration did not come to a halt with the opening of the former zonal border. It has rather been accompanied by a release of the cumulated migrant pressure from past decades. Initially, the fear and uncertainty that this new window of opportunity to flee the country might close again likely drove up migration figures.[45] In fact, following the first free elections since 1932, on 18th March in 1990, emigration started to show first tendencies of decline. The intension of the newly elected government to establish a fundament for the aspired reunification has been manifested in the introduction of the *social, economic and monetary union (SEMU)* on 1st July as well as the political reunification on 3rd October 1990. However,

44 See Schumann, K. F. (1996), pp. 33-34; Steiner, A. (2013), p. 38.
45 See Heiland, F. (2004), p. 176.

it did not take much time to discover that the German economy was in worse conditions than initially expected. In the wake of unification the economy was hardest hit by soaring wages, due to the bargaining efforts of western labour unions,[46] hence, increasing production cost, accompanied by a rapid decline in demand for East German products, which followed the vast appreciation of the currency.[47] As a consequence, East German GDP declined from 1989 to 1992 by approximately 30 percent and unemployment rates shot up from zero to over 15 percent of registered unemployed. If the individuals who transited into training schemes, early retirement and other newly introduced labour market schemes are taken into account, the fraction of jobless citizens even increased to 33 percent.[48] The deteriorating economic conditions exerted a consistent push on East German citizens to leave the country, which resulted in an outflow of approximately 870,000 migrants from January 1989 to January 1992, equalling an unfathomable ten percent of the local labour force, that is, five percent of the total population. Thereafter, migration began to stabilise at a yet considerable amount of 12,000 to 15,000 emigrants per month throughout 1992.[49]

The present analysis utilises this outstanding historical episode alongside its consequences for the East German economy to study the immigration impact through 1991 and 1992 on the West German property market. The analysis will be presented in the next two chapters of this thesis.

46 See Burda, M. C. and J. Hunt (2001), pp. 4-5.
47 See Akerlof, G. A. et al. (1991), p. 5.
48 See Burda, M. C. and J. Hunt (2001), pp. 1-2.
49 See Burda, C. (1993), p. 452.

3 Empirical Strategy and Data

The underlying chapter is partitioned into two central components to allow an elaboration on the methodological approach, employed to investigate the presence of a causal migration impact on local housing markets in West German destination economies. The empirical spatial correlation model is presented in Section 3.1, followed by an introduction of the related data sources alongside an incipient descriptive assessment, in Section 3.2.

3.1 Empirical Strategy

In order to estimate the impact of immigration on residential property prices, particularly rents in regional housing markets of western Germany, the following regression model is applied:

$$\Delta \log(rent_{j,c,1990-92}) = \beta_0 + \beta_1 m_{j,1991-92} + \beta_2 u_{j,1990} + \beta_3 \frac{arr_{j,1990}}{pop_{j,1990}} +$$

$$\beta_4 \Delta \log(arr_{j,1990-91}) + \mu_j + \rho_j + \varphi_j + \varepsilon_{j,1990-92} \qquad \text{(I)}$$

in which the dependent variable is the change in the log of rents between 1990 and 1992, observed for each metropolitan area *j* and rental category *c*, respectively. More specifically, rental prices refer to the end of year value on 31st December of each year and the three surveyed rental categories are the minimum, maximum and average first-use letting prices of newly built or renovated flats in Euro per square metre, henceforth referred to as *primary letting prices*. The main explanatory variable $m_{j,1991-92}$ is total immigration from East Germany received by destination *j* throughout 1991 and 1992, divided by metropolitan area *j*'s initial population in 1990, that is, prior to the surveyed immigration treatment. Due to the log-linear set up of this model, the coefficient of main interest, β_1, captures the effect of a one percentage point increase in the migrant share of the local population between any two points in time, on the change of rental prices over the surveyed time period, expressed in terms of percent. Moreover, since the immigration impact to destination *j* is measured as the total migrant inflow throughout 1991 to 1992 in relation to the a priory population stock in 1990, the interpretation of a percentage change in rents due to an immigration impact equal to one percentage point of the initial population intuitively coincides with the interpretation of a percentage change in rental prices due to an increase in destination *j*'s population by one percent arising from immigration.

In line with previous studies, the migration variable is in fact lagged in time, assuming that rental prices adjust rapidly to fundamental shifts in demand, as suggested by the stock-flow modelling approach typically applied in the field of housing market research. The underlying concept builds upon the fact that an initial stock of housing units is virtually fixed in the short-run, in that alterations in the capital stock involve enduring processes, as for example, construction and refurbishment activities. In comparison, property prices are highly flexible as housing markets are, in most instances, deregulated. Thus, property price adjustment constitutes the driving force in the equilibrating process induced by significant shifts in demand for housing due to, for instance, extraordinarily high immigration.[50] Furthermore, in the present study of primary let flats, the price setting power of landlords is supposedly even higher than that of the ones offering consecutively let flats in any one

50 See Smith, L. B. (1974), p. 481; Smith, L. B., Rosen, K. T. and G. Fallis (1988), p. 50.

housing market. Amongst other reasons, this is due to the fact that overall demand for newly constructed dwellings is usually higher and prices of newly-builts are more difficult to evaluate by prospective tenants. Moreover, previous studies on the development of internal migration following German reunification have shown that the largest proportion of the studied annual migrant streams relocated during the spring and summer period. Predominantly, peak migration months coincided with regular school breaks throughout each year.[51] Hence, since the observed rental price figures correspond to the end of year values and migrants arrived to the largest part by the beginning of autumn, rental prices supposedly underwent a considerable adjustment by then.

Due to the first-difference character of the regression equation, in which long-differences of the dependent rental price variables over a period of two subsequent years are investigated, that is, the entire time-span surveyed in the present study, destination specific time-invariant characteristics, which determine rental levels and are potentially correlated with migrants' location choices are differenced out.[52] Additionally, lagged values of time-variant location specific attributes and region specific dummy variables have been added as control variables. That is, the unemployment rate u_j in 1990 is included as a wealth indicating measure, as it is commonly argued that initial labour market conditions play an important role in determining migrants' relocation patterns.[53] Unfortunately, due to the restricted availability of data, the initial unemployment rate in 1990 is explored for the purpose of this thesis as opposed to more conclusive measures, such as the trend

51 See Grundmann, S. (1996 [1995]), pp. 4-7.
52 See Wooldridge, J. M. (2013), pp. 443-445.
53 See Saiz, A. (2007), p. 354.

development in unemployment rates over several years prior to migration, which may in fact be better suited controlling for differences in labour market conditions.

In contrast to seminal studies which explore several time-invariant characteristics, such as weather and other local amenities, in spite of the first difference set up of the respective models, the underlying study exploits a single variable that factually condenses a variety of those characteristics and arguably captures factors beyond the traditionally explored amenity measures.[54] The variable in perspective, $arr_{j,1990}$, is a tourism related indicator for attractiveness of a destination, and thus, an essential determinant of the corresponding housing market conditions and property prices therein. Precisely, $arr_{j,1990}$ covers the number of guest arrivals at local hospitality providers throughout the year 1990, and is further normalised by the destinations' population of the same year, as depicted by model equation (I). Indeed, this measure comprises a multitude of popularity features, as it summarises the total number of people with a purpose to visit an area, including both, professionally as well as privately motivated visits. Hence, the tourism variable mirrors on the one hand the scale of business activity, and on the other hand, amenities such as weather, surrounding landscape, architecture and sights among others. Moreover, the respective variable is included in the form of its log change between 1990 and 1991, in order to capture the trend development in the factors that drive business and pleasure tourism at the very beginning of the surveyed period. Accordingly, a positive trend in guest arrivals is interpreted as an indicator for an upbeat area featuring growing popularity, whereas a negative trend is applicable to a location characterised by slowing attractiveness. Again referring to the

[54] See Saiz, A. (2007), p. 354; Gonzalez, L. and F. Ortega (2013), p. 42.

restricted availability of data, the model is set up covering the trend development in guest arrivals from 1990 to 1991, whereupon the latter falls into the time period during which the immigration treatment is applied and might therefore yield further endogeneity bias. That is, migrants' arrival in 1991 might potentially be correlated with the trend development in guest arrivals due to, for instance, the attraction of visits from family and friends. Likewise, immigrants may further contribute to a change in the arrivals trend by stimulating business activity in the area. Nevertheless, the variable has been included in the present analysis, since the factual degree of migrant impact is assumed to be plausibly small, as migration does not, at least not immediately, alter fundamental characteristics of a destination area, such as weather, surrounding landscape and the like. Last, three types of dummy variables are included: The first set μ_j draws from the inference of four market type categories,[55] and the further two, denoted by ρ_j and φ_j, are region specific dummies, capturing for each metropolitan area which state it is located in and whether it is situated in the former inner German zonal border area. The characteristics of the market type and border area dummies will be discussed in more detail in Section 3.2. Moreover, the constant and of the idiosyncratic error term are denoted by β_0 and $\varepsilon_{j,1990-92}$, respectively.

The expected signs of the coefficient estimates of model (I) are listed in Table 1, indicating that the coefficient of β_1 is assumed to be positive, due to the fact that a migrant inflow raises the population and, thus, demand for residential properties, as long as the immigration impact does not induce an outflow of natives to the same extent or even over-proportionate outmigration. Interestingly, outmigration figures from

55 See bulwiengesa AG, RIWIS (2014b), supplementary material.

West Germany to the rest of the world experienced a dramatic increase in the years following reunification, whereas the surge may also have been accounted for by East-West migrants who further moved on internationally, subsequent to relocating to West Germany. Nevertheless, both effects mentioned are supportive of theories on potential spill-over effects of migration. However, such redistributive effects do presumably not instantly follow the arrival of immigrants in any specified market, and the likelihood that the outflow of inhabitants outweighs the preceding inflow is assumed to be low.[56]

Variable	$m_{j,1991-92}$	$u_{j,1990}$	$\frac{arr_{j,1990}}{pop_{j,1990}}$	$\Delta \log(arr_{j,1990-91})$	μ_j & ρ_j	φ_j
Exp. sign	(+)	(−)	(+)	(+)	(?)	(−)

Table 1: Expected Signs of Regression Coefficients [Author's representation based on own assessment.]

Despite the first-difference nature and the inclusion of the above mentioned controls, the estimation of model equation (I) may still suffer from endogeneity bias, due to self-selection of migrants into destination areas that show, under otherwise equal conditions, slower rental price growth, causing a downward bias in *Ordinary Least Squares (OLS)* estimates. Analogously, a merely coincidental influx of migrants to a certain area, which had recently gained considerable attractiveness for some reason and experiences high rental price growth, attributable to the boost in attractiveness, would overstate the effect of migration on rents. That is, the omission of such factors may cause OLS estimates to be upward biased.[57] Putting it differently, the potential correlation between $m_{j,1991-92}$ and $\varepsilon_{j,1990-92}$ violates the assumption of strict exogeneity of $m_{j,1991-92}$ rendering OLS estimates of the presented model biased,

56 See Card, D. (2001), p. 57; Gonzalez, L. and F. Ortega (2013), p. 42.
57 See Gonzalez, L. and F. Ortega (2013), pp. 42-43.

however, the direction of the bias is indeterminate without any further assessment.[58]

To circumvent this potential endogeneity problem, that is,

$$Cov(m_{j,1991-92}, \varepsilon_{j,1990-92}) \neq 0, \tag{II}$$

the present study employs an *instrumental variable* (IV) estimation approach, in which an instrument $\hat{z}_{j,1991-92}$ is constructed for $m_{j,1991-92}$, based on a theory that is plausibly exogenous to the observed rental outcome in the surveyed destination areas as well as the other variables in equation (I).[59] Consequently, following an approach employed in previous studies, a separate regression analysis of origin area characteristics, pushing migrants out of the surveyed origin regions, will be conducted in order to predict migration.[60]

Moreover, the created instrument is required to fulfil the identifying assumption that it is uncorrelated with the idiosyncratic error term:

$$Cov(\hat{z}_{j,1991-92}, \varepsilon_{j,1990-92}) = 0. \tag{III}$$

in addition to the exogeneity assumption in (III), the instrument needs to be carefully chosen in that it is sufficiently correlated with the endogenous explanatory variable, that is,

$$Cov(\hat{z}_{j,1991-92}, m_{j,1991-92}) \neq 0, \tag{IV}$$

and it must be relevant to explaining the observed variation in $m_{j,1991-92}$.

58 See Wooldridge, J. M. (2013), p. 445.
59 See loc. cit., pp. 491-492.
60 See Saiz, A. (2007), pp. 357-358; Frank, D. (2009), pp. 7-9.

There are two important aspects to the construction of an IV that require special attention: First, the exogeneity assumption in (III) cannot directly be tested due to the fact that the error term comprises factually unobserved characteristics. Thus, the selection of an appropriate instrument relies on the utilisation of a profound theory in order to justify the implied exogeneity.[61]

Second, the relevance assumption (IV) requires a sufficiently high correlation between instrument and endogenous explanatory variable; however, correlation is not automatically associated with causation. Consequently, a well-chosen instrument requires above a relatively high correlation a somewhat causal association with the endogenous explanatory variable, in order to allow for an identification of the causal effect of this variable on the observed outcome.[62] Both of these factors will be addressed in Section 3.2.4, in which the construction of the instrumental variable will be elaborated on.

To summarise, an instrument will be constructed for the purpose of conducting the underlying analysis, which features a causal association with the immigration variable; however, has no effect on the error term, such that, the only effect of the instrument on the log change in rents is exerted via an extraction of the causal effect of immigration on rents. Moreover, the causal effect will be identified in performing a standard *two-stage least squares* (2SLS) estimation, using $\hat{z}_{j,1991-92}$ as an instrument for $m_{j,1991-92}$, the results of which will be presented in Section 4.2.

61 See Wooldridge, J. M. (2013), p. 492.
62 See Cameron A. C. and Trivedi, P. K. (2009), pp. 95-97.

3.2 Data

Part 3.2 is divided into four subsections in accordance with the explored data sources. In Section 3.2.1, a geographical categorisation of the investigative units will be established. A summary of related trends in German internal East-West migration is provided in Section 3.2.2, followed by Section 3.2.3, in which a descriptive assessment of trends in property prices, material to the period studied, is depicted. In the last subsection of this part, characteristic data on the surveyed origin areas will be presented in alignment with the underlying concepts that are utilised in the instrument creation. Moreover, the results of the corresponding auxiliary regression analysis will be summarised.

3.2.1 Geography

From a geographical point of view, the two major units of analysis which are distinguished in the underlying investigation relate, on the one hand, to the East German territory of the former GDR, sending migrants, and on the other hand, to the West German region, specifically metropolitan areas thereof, receiving migrants. More precisely, the recipient areas in the West encompass 72 metropolitan units which have been selected according to the following criteria: RIWIS bulwiengesa AG, henceforth RIWIS, provided data on 127 German cities, out of which Berlin and 25 cities of the former GDR have been dropped. Moreover, solely those western cities that were classified as *Kreisfreie Staedte* (urban districts) throughout the surveyed period were chosen. These are separate entities, featuring self-contained municipal structures and clear cut borders at the district level. The selection criterion stems from two reasons: First, the sole analysis of those independent urban municipal unions allows a highly precise matching of the underlying migration data to the destination areas, since the smallest entity common to both data sets is the district level. Any matching of immigration streams on the district level to metropolitan units that do not constitute urban districts, however, are merely part of a rural district, would lead to an overestimation of the immigration impact to the metropolitan unit. In order to demonstrate the importance of measuring the migrant inflow into a destination unit as accurately as possible, the case of the metropolitan area Fuerth in Bavaria may be considered: The respective urban district was characterised by 103,362 inhabitants in 1990. In the underlying analysis the migrant inflow to the metropolitan district during 1991 to '92 amounted to 901 people, accounting for an immigration impact of approximately 0.87 percent. Moreover, an additional 773 migrants were destined for the respective evenly named rural district. If taken into account, the total immigrant inflow into the urban district and the surrounding rural area amounted to 1674, or 1.62 percent, respectively.[63] Hence, including immigration to the surrounding rural district, an overly high immigration impact would be attributed to the city of Fuerth. This example illustrates an effect that may be replicated onto any destination unit which does not constitute a separate metropolitan district in itself, and consequently, the corresponding immigration data cannot be accurately attributed to.

Second, the intension of restricting the destination sample to urban districts is further motivated by the consistent provision of secondary data among those investigative units. Notwithstanding, the secondary data were also provided by RIWIS and are an essential prerequisite to the proceeding analysis of the West German property market. Accordingly, this reduces the number of surveyed destination units to 72 metropolitan areas. A complete list of the individual observation units,

---

63 See bulwiengesa AG, RIWIS (2014a); German Federal Statistical Office (2014), datasets.

alongside selected key characteristics, is provided in Table A.1 in the annex. Analogously, the summary statistics for those characteristics are shown in Table 2, depicting that initial destination unit population in 1990 ranges from 44,246 to 1,652,363 inhabitants; whereas the immigration treatment to those areas ranges from 160 to 11,121 people from 1991 to '92, or analogously, from 0.135 to 2.344 percent of the initial population.

	Obs	**Mean**	**Std. Dev.**	**Min**	**Max**
Population (1990)	72	261162.7	271192	44246	1652363
Immigrants (1991-'92)*	72	1494.444	1833.697	160	11121
Immigration impact (%)**	72	.6147534	.3342001	.1345261	2.343715

Notes: * Cumulated immigration from East Germany as of 1991 & '92.
** (Immigrants/ 1990 population).

Table 2: Destination Regions - West German Metropolitan Areas (Summary Statistics) [Data on West German urban districts obtained from bulwiengesa AG, RIWIS (2014a). Immigration data obtained from German Federal Statistical Office (2014)]

Another important geographical consideration is related to the manifestation of the former zonal border area, prior to reunification. In particular, the urban districts that were located closely to this region may require different treatment in the analysis. This is mainly due to the fact that these areas were major recipients of subsidies prior to, and in many instances, also after reunification.[64] In addition to the extensive subsidisation programmes, the proximity to the origin regions presumably entailed substantial commuter inflows from the East, partly replacing immigration. Likewise, emigration streams out of these areas may have been disproportionately high in comparison to the non-border zone districts. On the one hand, the latter effect may be driven by

[64] See Frank, D. (2009), p. 12.

traditional pull factors, such as relatively low living costs in the East and other motives of West German natives to emigrate. On the other hand, increased competitive pressures due to the participation of East Germans on, for instance, the local labour market may have likewise exhibited a push effect on natives out of the western border region. Accordingly, the column *Zonal Border Region* of Table A.1 indicates which urban districts are located in this extraordinary area.

The selection of the respective investigative units follows from an extensive study on the economic development in the zonal border region by Redding and Sturm in 2008. They survey a balanced panel dataset composed of 119 West German cities with a population of over 20,000 inhabitants in 1919, covering the time period from 1919 up until 2002 and identify 20 cities located in the inner German border region. More precisely, the 20 border area cities are defined as being located within 75 kilometre of *Great Circle Distance* from their nearest point along the former internal border.[65] Since, the 72 urban districts examined in the present investigation represent a subsample of the afore-mentioned study, out of those 20 cities 13 investigative units are represented. After careful consideration, Hamburg was excluded from the suggested list due to its status as an independent state and important hub for international trade, which reduces the number of observation units that are classified as border region districts to twelve, as shown in Table A.1. Moreover, the respective scholars find that cities situated in the West German border region have been characterised by substantially lower population growth than corresponding cities which are located farther from the zonal border.[66] Prevailingly, main explanations for this development are suggested to be traced back to a series of economic

---

65 See Redding, S. J. and D. M. Sturm (2008), pp. 1775-1776.
66 See loc. cit., p. 1766.

distortions in those areas since the implementation of the border, which jointly acted in reducing real wages. This development induced West German population movements out of the affected area, triggering a real wage equalisation process, alongside which a downward pressure on prices of non-traded goods was exerted.[67] The latter effect, establishes a crucial insight in relation to the proceeding study of the West German property market.

Turning to migrants' origin areas in the East, the former division of the GDR territory comprised 15 administrative districts, which were subdivided into 27 urban districts, 189 rural districts and 11 boroughs of East Berlin. With the onset of German reunification an extensive process of administrative restructuring was initiated. The establishment of the five newly formed German states and the merge of East with West Berlin went hand in hand with major redistricting activities and the imposition of 38 employment office districts, each of which encompasses several urban and rural districts.[68] The analysis conducted in the present thesis exploits the introduction of the EODs, since the elementary grouping of districts that are adjacent to each other does not alter the district level borders. It rather implies aggregated investigative entities, featuring a combination of clear cut borders on the district level. Thence, the district level emigration data can be precisely determined, combined and allocated to distinct *EOD origin regions*. In result, this approach allows to most precisely analyse and describe where migrants originate from, conducting both the OLS and IV approach, since the smallest unit for which consistent secondary data on origin characteristics are provided is the EOD level. The composition of the EODs in the present analysis builds upon a detailed study on the

---

67 See Redding, S. J. and D. M. Sturm (2008), p. 1774.

68 See Rudolph, H. (1990), p. 474.

characteristics of the newly formed local labour markets in eastern Germany, by Helmut Rudolph in 1990. However, the four separate EODs of former East Berlin have been merged to one, reducing the number of migrant sending regions on the EOD level to 35 investigative units. Crucial to the present analysis of the entire range of EODs is that major district reforms have been introduced from 1993 onwards reducing the number of East German districts from 215 to 111 in 1996.[69] Since these reforms did not come into effect during the time period studied, the migration data can be matched with the EODs without any further requirement to merge districts and reduce the number of surveyed origin areas, as presented in similar studies.[70] A detailed list of the EOD composition on the district level is provided in Table A.2.1, followed by Table A.2.2, presenting an overview of selected origin area characteristics.[71] Moreover, the related summary statistics are compiled in Table 3, depicting that the initial population on 30th September 1989, that is, prior to reunification, ranged from 87,445 to 721,325 inhabitants across the EODs, whereas total emigration during 1991 and '92 ranged from 4,292 to 25,091 people or 2.83 to 9.03 percent of the initial population, respectively. The sizeable outflow of migrants throughout the surveyed period clearly prevails, representing on average 4.95 percent of the origin population prior to reunification. Moreover, the 35 origin regions range in terms of size from 404 to 8,482 square kilometres.

In addition, Appendix Table A.2.2 reveals that certain origin units have been marked as border regions, which may analogously require special treatment for the reasons discussed above and beyond. For instance,

---

69 See Goebel, J. (2011), pp. 2-3.
70 See Frank, D. (2009), pp. 45-48.
71 See Rudolph, H. (1990), pp. 487-489.

these areas benefitted from an enormous increase in centrality, thus, increased investment activity and likely better perspectives for the labour market development than other origin areas in perspective. At the same

	Obs	Mean	Std. Dev.	Min	Max
Initial working population*	35	253825.2	127806.3	87445	721325
Area (sqkm)	35	3095.457	2141.5	404	8482
Emigration (1991-'92)**	35	12160.91	5328.313	4292	25091
Emigration impact (%)***	35	4.953351	1.011767	2.830624	9.030444
Distance to West German urban district (km)+	2520	357.8256	116.6091	42.92701	792.3284

Notes: * Refers to working population prior to reunification, precisely 30/09/1989.
** Cumulated outmigration as of 1991 & '92 from each EOD to West Germany, i.e. to the surveyed metropolitan areas and beyond.
*** (Emigrants 1991-'92)/ working population (30/09/1989).
+ Ellipsoidal distances of any pairwise combination of origin and destination geographic (reference) centre.

Table 3: Origin Regions - East German Employment Office Districts (Summary Statistics) [Data on initial EOD characteristics adapted from Rudolph, H. (1990), pp. 487-489. Emigration data obtained from German Federal Statistical Office (2014).]

time, increased centrality was followed by a transportation surge and traffic through those regions, for which the required infrastructure was not present. Hence, much of the traffic was directed at the rural roads, reducing life quality in villages and small towns located at those gateways to the west. The various overlaying effects in the origin locations close to the former border area, pose a challenge to predicting whether border location exerts an overall dampening or accelerating effect on emigration, if any at all. In order to investigate the question in perspective, all EODs adjacent to West Germany as well as East Berlin have been allocated border region status.

Finally, since part of the underlying IV estimation strategy exploits the suggested effect that proximity yields on the magnitude of migrant streams between any origin and destination region, the respective distances need to be determined.[72] In order to accomplish that, data on coordinates of the geographical centres of the 72 destination cities in the West as well as geographical reference points of the 35 origin areas in the East have been gathered using the web based application *GeoHack*, which is part of the *WikiProject* on geo-referencing.[73] With regards to determining the geographical reference centres of the 35 EODs, the coordinates of the urban or rural district with the highest initial population have been obtained, which was in most instances equal to the administrative centre of the EODs. Each chosen reference point for the corresponding EOD is listed in column *Geo Reference Centre* of annex Table A.2.2. The coordinates relate to the World Geodetic System of 1984 (WGS 84) and refer to the given state in 2014; however, the deviations of the present coordinates from the actual coordinates in 1991 are assumed to be negligibly small. This is due to the fact that ellipsoidal distances are applied in the present study and the location of each geographical centre is unlikely to have significantly changed. Nevertheless, even if driving distances were used, deviations are presumably small, since major motorways and railroads were already present at the beginning of the 1990s. The ellipsoidal distances of any pairwise combination of sending and recipient areas represent 2,520 combinations and are calculated using the *Stata*® application *geodist*. The corresponding summary statistics are further presented in Table 3. Out of the 2,520 possible distances, linking origin and destination districts, the average distance amounts to approximately 358 kilometres;

---

72 See Ravenstein, E. G. (1885), pp. 198-199.
73 See GeoHack (2014).

where the range between shortest and farthest distance reaches from 43 kilometres till close to 800 kilometres.

3.2.2 German East-West Migration

The dramatic series of political events in the late history of the GDR, discussed in Section 2.1, which resulted in the fall of the Berlin Wall on 9th November 1989, immediately induced an enormous exodus of former GDR citizens to West Germany. More precisely, the huge build-up of migration potential has become evident in the outflow of approximately 1,232,652 emigrants form 1989 to 1992. In fact, the strict enforcement of travel and relocation restrictions applicable to GDR residents since the construction of the Berlin Wall in 1961, and therewith, the ultimate manifestation of the *Iron Curtain*, reduced emigration of East Germans to comparably negligible quantities over more than quarter of a century, as shown in Figure 1. The release of this excess migrant pressure resulted in a historical peaking point of close to 400,000 emigrants during 1989 as well as 1990.[74] These figures outnumbered even the total outmigration figures in the years short before the construction of the Wall as well as the year of the uprising on 17th June 1953.[75] Moreover, the outflow of East Germans throughout the period of 1989 to 1992 corresponds to roughly 7.5 percent of the former GDR citizens or analogously, 11.7 percent of the working age population in 1989.[76] Although annual outmigration subsequently declined to 249,743 and 199,170 people in 1991 and 1992, and further stabilised at on average 168 thousand annual emigrants over the following four years, the persistency of East-West migration prevailed. Moreover, while West-

[74] See German Federal Statistical Office (2000), dataset; Grundmann, S. (1996 [1995]), p. 3.

[75] See Schumann, K. F. (1996), p. 15.

[76] See Fritz, W. (2001 [2004]), dataset.

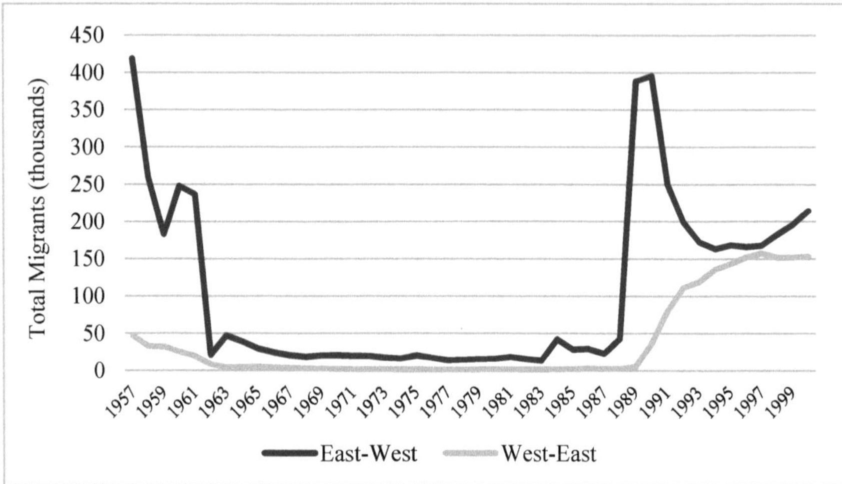

Figure 1: German Internal Migration 1957-2000 [Author's representation adapted from German Federal Statistical Office (2000).]

East migration significantly increased throughout the early to mid-1990s, net outmigration from the area remained positive, as illustrated in Figure 1. Moreover, the migrant population was mainly represented by working age migrants.[77] As a consequence, the particularly high proportion of relatively young working age emigrants thereof raised immediate concerns of a brain drain from East Germany.[78]

In addition, another emigration surge has been denoted from 1997 onwards, peaking at 1.64 percent of the East German population in 2001, accordingly reaching levels close to the ones of 1991 and 1992. The second emigration wave was likely due to deteriorating economic conditions in the East, such as worsening employment prospects following the short period of stabilisation during 1994 to '95. Altogether, the P&P structure in the German internal migration scenario

[77] See German Federal Statistical Office (2000), dataset.
[78] See Burda, M. C. (1993), p. 458.

has been altered several times throughout the 1990s: On the one hand, emigration slowed down due to the increasing optimism and speedy wage convergence in the east, versus shrinking employment prospects in the western part of the country, as Germany followed West Europe into recession. On the other hand, a reversal of the conditions in the West combined with an ongoing deterioration of the Eastern economy in the late 1990s stimulated an emigration resurge.[79]

Focusing at the migration corridors of East-West migration since unification, that is, where migrants originated from as well as their distribution across the west, a main challenge to a consistent analysis is posed by a feature of the regime change itself, which was expressed in the collapse of the former GDR administrative structures. Accordingly, the collapse of the GDR institutional framework was followed by a transition period, throughout which the respective duties were reassigned to the corresponding West German officiating bodies. Hence, particularly during the early transition process in 1989 and 1990, analytical documentation lacks multitudinous inconsistencies, which is equally applicable to internal migration data. In order to overcome this challenge, a study by Frank Heiland in 2004 has been devoted to a consistent replication of state level trends in East-West migration from 1989 to 2002. In order to accomplish that, he jointly analyses data from the former GDR citizen residence registry, *Zentrales Einwohnerregister Berlin-Biesdorf (ZER)*, which ceased data collection in 1992, as well as, the German Federal Statistical Office, which collects the district level migration data for entire Germany, including the new states in the East, from 1991 onwards. The data refers to all German inhabitants throughout any year in perspective, as it is a legal requirement to any German

79 See Heiland, F. (2004), pp. 176-178.

citizen to register any change of residency with the local officiating authorities.[80] As noted by several scholars, the data of the two sources differ substantially for the years commonly surveyed. In particular, the ZER data reports significantly lower outmigration levels for the years 1991 and 1992, than the German Federal Statistical Office.[81] Nevertheless, the distribution of migrants across West German destinations largely coincides among the two datasets.[82] Figure 2, depicts the harmonised aggregated outmigration rates in terms of initial population for the five newly formed Eastern states from 1989 to 2002. The peaking point for the state Saxony was reached immediately after the fall of the Berlin Wall in 1989, at approximately 2.3 percent of the region's population, moreover representing the highest overall outmigration rate amongst all states throughout the surveyed time frame. The outmigration rates across the remaining states peaked in 1990, with Saxony still ranking third after Saxony-Anhalt and Thuringia denoting 2.3 and 2.2 percent respectively. Analogously, the top ranking recipient states in the West both in 1989 and 1990 were Bavaria and Baden-Wuerttemberg followed by North-Rhine-Westphalia and Lower-Saxony. Moreover, the origin areas that were characterised by the highest propensity to migrate shifted in a clockwise direction from 1989 onwards, beginning with Saxony in the south-eastern part of the former GDR. Whereas migration did not seem to follow a certain pattern at the very early stages in 1989, relocation choices increasingly showed proximity related tendencies in the subsequent years.[83] Therefore, the consideration of proximity's role in shaping migrant streams in the present analysis is further supported.

---

80 See Heiland, F. (2004), p. 174.
81 See Grundmann, S. (1996 [1995]), p. 4.
82 See Heiland, F. (2004), p. 190.
83 See loc. cit., pp. 177-185; Grundmann, S. (1996 [1995]), pp. 12-15.

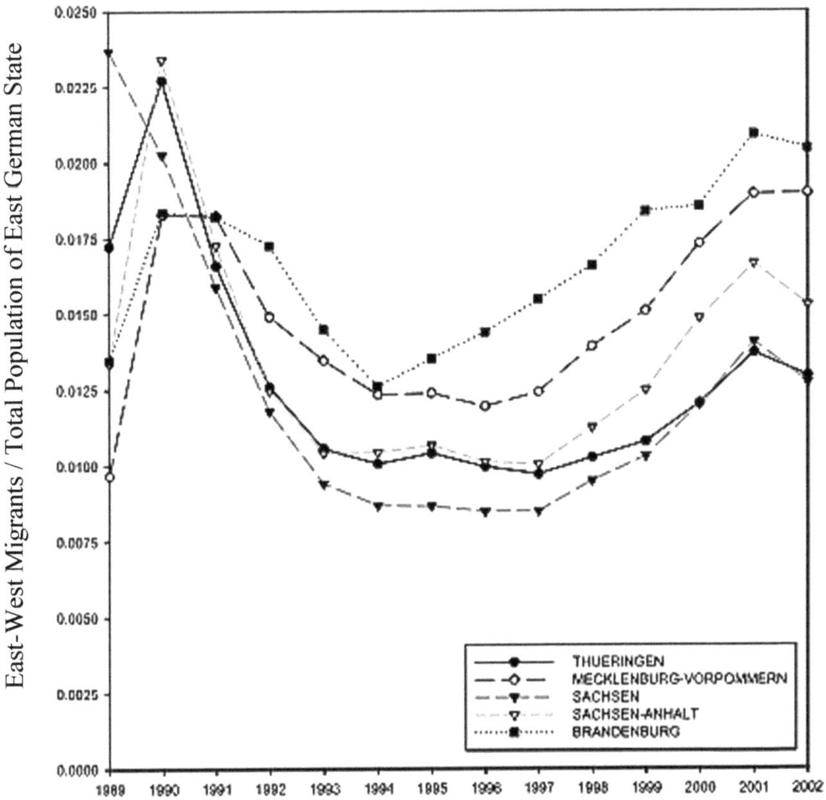

Figure 2: Aggregated Outmigration Rates by Origin Region [Heiland, F. (2004), p. 179.]

Accordingly, in Figure 3 the distribution of the total emigrant volume during 1991 and '92 across the origin regions in perspective is outlined. The data has been extracted from the district level migration matrices of the years 1991 and 1992, which were provided by the German Federal Statistical Office. The figures represent the entire migration flows towards West Germany, that is, emigration destined for the 72 surveyed urban districts and beyond. However, West Berlin is excluded, as some of the migrant streams to the city's recipient boroughs were not precisely identified in the matrices. Although the migration structures in 1991 and '92 were more distance oriented by then, the top ranking recipient areas remained unchanged. Nonetheless, the overall allocation across states started to be more balanced since 1992. With reference to the right-hand-side scale of Figure 3, each origin state's share of total emigrants destined for any one of the 72 surveyed metropolitan areas is shown. Thus, the surveyed sample represents roughly 25 to 35 percent of the total East-West migration.[84]

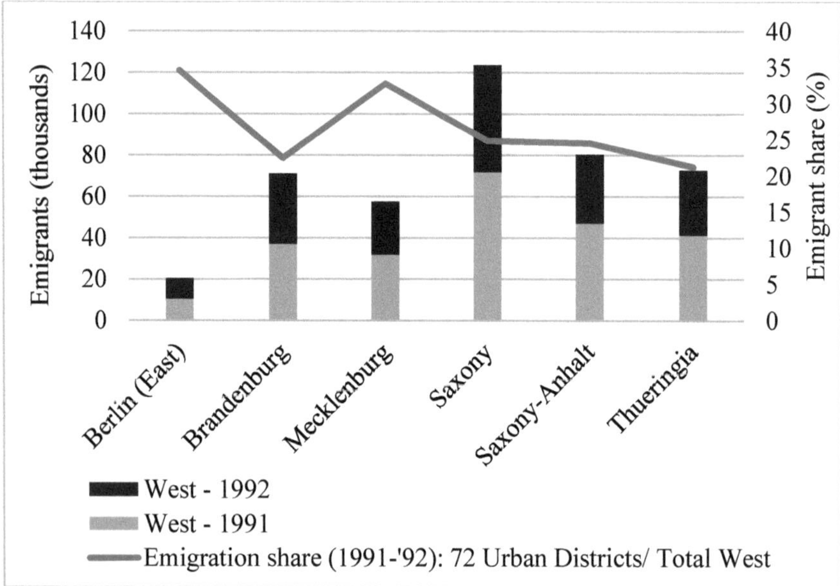

Figure 3: Emigration from East to West Germany 1991-1992 (excluding West Berlin) [Author's representation adapted from German Federal Statistical Office (2014).]

A more detailed overview of the surveyed destination regions is represented in Figure 4, which depicts cumulated outmigration to West Germany from 1991 to 1992, for each of the 35 sending EODs.

[84] See German Federal Statistical Office (2014), dataset; Heiland, F. (2004), p. 177.

Figure 4: Emigration from Employment Office Districts to West Germany 1991-1992 (excluding West Berlin)

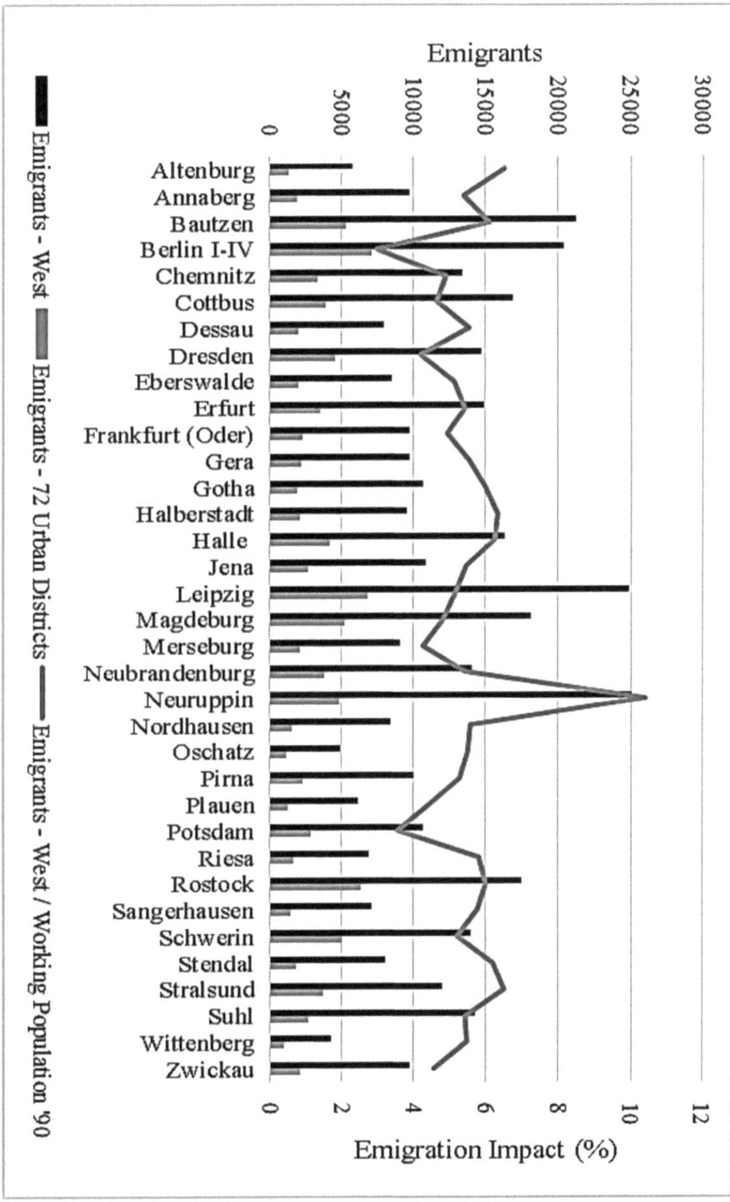

[Author's representation adapted from German Federal Statistical Office (2014), dataset; Koller, M. and T. Jung-Hammon (1993), p. 9.]

Analogously, the light grey bars represent the corresponding figures on outmigration to the 72 destination districts of the present analysis. The represented share of urban migration to the 72 areas in terms of total West migration ranges from 17.7 to 36.3 percent, indicating that the investigated sample represents on average 24.5 percent of the entire emigrant population. Moreover, the emigration impact to the EODs varied substantially, as represented by the line graph with reference to the right-hand-side scale. More specifically, the share of accumulated West-migrants from 1991 to '92, expressed in terms of initial working population at the end of November 1990, ranged from approximately three to 10.4 percent. Hence, the average emigration impact to the 35 EODs amounted to 5.46 percent, whereat the large deviations among the figures give rise to the suspicion that in certain EODs East German citizens have faced stronger incentives to migrate than others, which is subject to a more detailed discussion presented in Section 3.2.4 in the proceedings of this thesis.[85] The corresponding immigration impact rates for the 72 destination units are listed in Table A.1 in the annex, ranging from 0.13 to 2.3 percent. Due to the fact that the remaining analysis builds upon an investigation of factors, exogenous to rental prices in West Germany, that potentially drove emigration and allow to most accurately describe the migrant streams between the surveyed origin and destination regions, the individual district level streams have been extracted from the migration matrices and aggregated over time and space. Precisely 2520 individual streams, that is one stream for each pairwise combination of origin and destination units, are obtained by aggregating district level emigration to EOD level, as presented in annex

[85] See German Federal Statistical Office (2014), dataset; Koller, M. and T. Jung-Hammon (1993), p. 9.

Table A.2. Furthermore, the respective values for 1991 and '92 are added and matched with their respective destination.

3.2.3 West German Property Market

In order to analyse the reaction of residential property prices in West Germany to the sudden and extraordinarily high immigrant inflow from the eastern parts of the country in the wake of reunification, data have been obtained from RIWIS bulwiengesa AG. RIWIS is a commercial property price analyst, engaging for over 30 years in extensive data collection and analysis of property markets, in order to provide indices for various residential and commercial market segments throughout Germany. The data provided by RIWIS constitutes an exceptional collation of consistent information on German regional property markets, and is therefore a widely accepted source of information, exploited by various established institutions, such as the *Organisation for Economic Co-operation and Development (OECD)* and the German Central Bank, to create internationally comparable indices for the purpose of monitoring the development of the country-wide housing market over time.[86] The RIWIS database provides relatively limited housing market data for 60 cities in West Germany since 1975. However, it features consistent annual data for 125 East and West German cities since 1990. In particular, the extracted subset of housing prices and secondary data provided by RIWIS for the purpose of conducting the present investigation refers to annual data on the development of residential rental and property purchasing prices from 1990 to 1995, whereby the respective data for 1990 to 1993 have been explored in the regression analysis. This is due to the fact that the immigration impact during the years 1991 to '92 is the applied treatment and property prices are highly

86 See Kholodilin, K. et al. (2014), p. 1232.

flexible, thus, tend to respond rapidly to alterations in supply and demand conditions.[87]

The technique RIWIS employs with regards to data collation builds upon a continuously updated and revised data base, empirical research, test purchases, surveys and questionnaires as well as independent auditing processes, among others.[88] Moreover, the available rental prices are classified according to newly built or refurbished flats, that is a *primary let*, and flats that have been previously let, henceforth denoted by *secondary let*. The average size of a typical surveyed unit corresponds to a two bedroom apartment, referred to as a *three room flat* according to German estate terminology, which comprises approximately 65 to 95 square metres of living space. The corresponding prices are expressed as gross nominal rental values per square metre and moreover distinguished between minimum, average and maximum rents. Notably, the minimum and maximum values do not refer to the ultimate top- or bottom-rents *per se*, however, illustrate an average value of the observation units in the top or bottom three to five percent quantile, accordingly. Likewise, the average rental price does not replicate an arithmetic average, median or modus in mathematical terms. It rather illustrates typical average level rents, commonly observable in the particular market. Furthermore, all annual property price levels present the values on 31st December of the respective year. Accordingly, the secondary data on market characteristics provided by RIWIS refer to either annual average values or annual total values of the calendar year in perspective. With regards to the destination characteristics explored in the regression analysis, the population figures relate to annual values on 31st December, unemployment rates replicate the annual average and the tourism control

[87] See Smith, L. B., Rosen, K. T. and G. Fallis (1988), p. 50.
[88] See bulwiengesa AG, RIWIS (2015), p. 1.

variable refers to the sum of guest arrivals, that is, the number of guests who checked-in at local accommodation providers throughout the surveyed year. In addition, RIWIS defined four property market type categories, in terms of size and functionality of the surveyed locations. These categories are time-invariant throughout the surveyed period, allowing to cluster the metropolitan areas according to their importance as functional centres on a local, regional, national or international scale.[89]

In the remainder of this section, the evolution of the German property market index will be presented in order to build a foundation for the proceeding analysis. Accordingly, an illustration of the RIWIS property index from 1975 to 2014 is presented in Figure 5. Until 1990, the related figures refer solely to West Germany, indicating a continuous upward trend in the level of property prices since 1975. From 1990 the development of property prices in the East German part of the country is included. Taking a first glance at the index trend development for the first four years preceding reunification reveals a substantial surge in

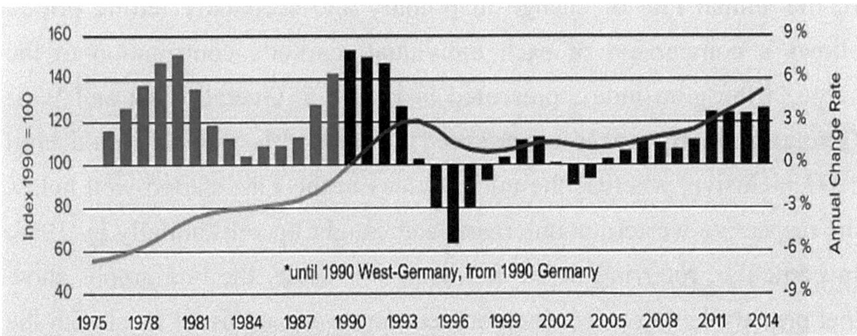

Figure 5: German Property Index and Annual Rate of Change, 1975-2014 [bulwiengesa AG, RIWIS (2015), p. 1.]

89 See bulwiengesa AG, RIWIS (2014b), supplementary material.

property prices. Moreover, the annual rates of change in property prices have increased strongly since 1989, coinciding with the first major immigrant wave at the time. Indeed, the annual rate of change in property prices reached a peaking point in 1991 at roughly eight percent, trumping even the highest rates observed in the years following the oil price shocks in the 1970s.

Although the surge in German property prices prevails, it remains unclear whether a substantial part of this development is attributable to the immigration impact to the West German housing market or other driving forces, such as the economic upturn during the observed period. In addition, the increase in the joint index values for East and West Germany further poses a challenge to the evaluation of the particular trend development in the West, as the East German market experienced a dramatic increase in property prices with the onset of the unification process.[90] Therefore, a summary of the rental price evolution from 1990 to 1995 of the distinct markets is presented in Figure 6. Employing the provided indices for the average values in the variables of interest, that is, the annual rate of change in primary and secondary letting prices, allows a comparison of each individual market's contribution to the surge in the joint index, presented in Figure 5. Overall, East and West German property prices experienced a remarkable growth period until 1993 inclusive; whereas the initial values in the East started well below the respective western counterparts and caught up substantially by 1994. In particular, referring to the left-hand-side scale, the line graphs show that primary letting prices in East Germany were almost at level with the West German analogue, at approximately 7.50 Euro per square metre in 1994. Unsurprisingly and in line with the speedy price convergence,

[90] See Sachverständigenrat (1993), p. 93.

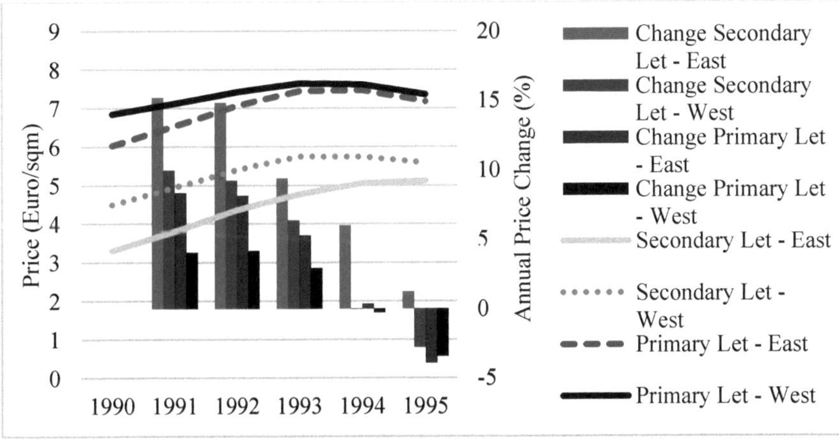

Figure 6: Development of Average Rental Prices in former East vs. West Germany, 1990-1995 [Adapted from bulwiengesa AG, RIWIS (2014), dataset.]

the annual rates of change in the East German primary letting prices, denoted by the corresponding bar chart figures marked on the right-hand-side, lie on average roughly two percentage points above the western rates. Analogously, the observed annual rates of change in rental prices of secondary lets lie approximately five percentage points above the West German equivalent. Nevertheless, focusing exclusively on the West German market, an exceptional surge in property prices becomes evident throughout the surveyed period of the proceeding analysis. In particular, whether and to what extend this development is attributable to immigration will be explored in Section 4 of this thesis.

3.2.4 Origin Characteristics and Instrument Construction

Instrumental variable estimation techniques are widely used in empirical research, as these applications are regarded a powerful tool in overcoming endogeneity problems associated with omitted variables and measurement errors.[91] Accordingly, an IV approach will be applied in the present study in order to mitigate associated problems conducting OLS estimation of model (I), as discussed in Section 3.1. More precisely, the underlying study constructs an instrumental variable following the seminal approaches of Albert Saiz, who conducts a panel random effects estimation in order to account for immigration to the United States based on various origin country characteristics;[92] and Douglas Frank, who applies a similar approach to predict migration from East German origin areas using labour market indicators for unemployment and quality of available jobs.[93]

Analogously, the present analysis attempts to predict migration employing a separate regression model that exploits exclusively origin characteristics of the surveyed 35 EODs, which constitute driving forces in pushing out migrants from East Germany. Most importantly and crucial to the analysis, the explored push factors are perspicuously exogenous to the observed outcomes in the western housing markets. Furthermore, the distances between the surveyed origin areas and the destination cities in the West are utilised to describe the distribution of migrants across the western metropolitan areas, which are by nature exogenously given and commonly applied in migration research, since first denoted a crucial determinant of migrant streams, in the 19th

[91] See Angrist, J. D. and A. B. Krueger (2001), pp. 71-73.
[92] See Saiz, A. (2007), pp. 357-358.
[93] See Frank, D. (2009), pp. 7-24.

century.[94] The exploitation of the exogenous variation in push factors across the individual origin areas builds upon a theory of international trade, particularly the production of export goods in the host economy. As discussed in Chapter 2, the East German economy was in various aspects negatively affected by the transition process from the structures of a centrally planned economy to an open market economy. Apart from inefficient production processes, an obsolete capital stock and rapidly rising production costs in the wake of wage convergence to West German levels,[95] the East German export industry, a major economic driving force of the GDR and important source of external funding, suffered substantially.[96] A possible explanation for the latter development is that specialisation according to comparative advantages and learning processes were factually impeded on the grounds that GDR exports were prevailingly oriented towards the *COMECON (Council for Mutual Economic Assistance)* states, accounting for close to 50 percent of the foreign trade volume, half of which was conducted with the Soviet Union based on formal contracts on the bilateral exchange of goods and resources.[97] More specifically, right before the introduction of the Social Economic and Monetary Union the proportion of GDR exports to the COMECON states amounted to approximately 75 percent.[98] West Germany solely acted as a denotative western GDR trade partner;[99] however, mainly due to the West German imports of crude oil, which the GDR was granted access at discounted rates via the Soviet Union as a part of the above mentioned trade agreement.[100] The remainder of GDR

94 See Ravenstein, E. G. (1885), pp. 198-199.
95 See Sachverständigenrat (1991), p. 70.
96 See loc. cit., p. 77.
97 See Stehn, J. and H. Schmieding (1990), p. 60-61.
98 See Sachverständigenrat (1991), p. 77.
99 See Stehn, J. and H. Schmieding (1990), p. 61.
100 See Ahrens, R. (2013), p. 174.

foreign trade was at most unsystematically spread across the *Organisation for European Economic Co-operation (OEEC)* states and other western parts of the world.[101] As a result, the eastern part of the country was hit by the expiration of the agreements with the COMECON states since the GDR virtually ceased to exist with the establishment of the reunified Germany.[102] The contractual agreement of the "program for specialisation and cooperation in production between the GDR and USSR until 1990"[103] was initiated in 1979 and featured a list of tradable goods both partners were obliged to deliver on an annual basis. As a consequence, the GDR export sector predominantly specialised in the field of mechanical engineering, such as shipbuilding and vehicle construction as well as the production of machine tools, chemical installation and equipment for the textile and publishing industries.[104] To summarise, with the introduction of the economic and monetary union on 1st July 1990, the East German Mark was replaced by the West German D-Mark with a specified 1:1 adjustment rate for prices and wages, which however, led to an actual estimated appreciation of the currency by approximately 350 percent within a few days and induced an abrupt decline in demand for East German export goods.[105] Particularly, the COMECON states were unable to maintain the trading partnership, previously established with the GDR, due to the regime change from an internal clearing system for foreign trade among those states, based on the inconvertible Valuta Mark or transferable Rouble, to convertible currencies.[106]

---

101 See Stehn, J. and H. Schmieding (1990), pp. 60-63.
102 See Ahrens, R. (2013), p. 175.
103 Stehn, J. and H. Schmieding (1990), p. 74, translated by the author.
104 See Meier, C. (1986), pp. 93-120.
105 See Heiland, F. (2004), p. 191; Akerlof, G. A. et al. (1991), pp. 8-9.
106 See Ahrens, R. (2013), p. 175.

The present study exploits this characteristic shock to the East German export industry via the construction of indicators, measuring the impact to the migrant sending regions arising from sectors that were amongst the hardest hit by the export related production declines. Complying with the GDR export oriented production discussed above, the majority of export goods was concentrated in the manufacturing sectors, particularly processed goods thereof as well as the chemical industry. Indeed, the respective sectors have experienced dramatic declines in net production since the introduction of the SEMU. That is, from mid-1990 to 1991 net production in the chemical sector declined by 21.9 percent, whereas production in the machinery and vehicle manufacturing sector declined by 48.4 percent and in the electro-technical sector by 52.3 percent. Notably, these declines were further facilitated in 1992, with the exception of the electro-technical sector, for which the production remained resilient from 1991 to 1992.[107] In order to calculate comparable indices, which measure the impact of each sector specific production decline on the sending district level, data on the sectoral workforce distribution of the 35 EODs have been obtained from a study of the regional labour market compositions, which is based on the *Berufstaetigenerhebung (BTE)* by the former GDR central administration office for statistics, from 30th September 1989. Therefore, the data replicate the *status quo* sectoral structure in each EOD prior to unification, and therewith, preceding the shock to the export industry. More specifically, the former GDR classification of 43 industrial branches has been translated into 21 economic sectors, for each of which the respective employment share has been provided on the district level according to the redistricting state in 1990.[108] Since the sector shares are

---

[107] See Sachverständigenrat (1993), p. 375.
[108] See Rudolph, H. (1990), pp. 474-477.

inferred from the relative employment concentration across sectors for each EOD, the shock indicators may be interpreted as a hazard rate or push factor of labour migration out of the area in perspective. Moreover, due to the character of the centrally planned economy and the GDR's specialisation in the production of export goods, the sectoral distribution was highly slanted towards specific regions. In fact, many districts with very high sector concentration, predominantly applicable to the chemical industry, were classified as mono-structured labour market regions.[109] Thence, the shock impact varied significantly across sectors as well as EODs.

For each sector and investigated origin region the export industry shock indicators are calculated as follows:

$$impact_{k,i} = sector\ share_{k,i} \times production\ decline_k \times \frac{working\ pop_{i,1990}}{working\ pop_{GDR,1990}}, \qquad (V)$$

where $impact_{k,i}$ denotes the shock impact to sending district i, arising from local concentration of sector k, with $k \in \{machine,\ electro,\ chemical\}$, weighted by the affected working population in terms of total GDR working population. The corresponding figures for sector share and production decline[110] are expressed in terms of percent. Notably, the population data refers to the working population in November 1990,[111] that is, short before the dramatic production decline was triggered by the break down in demand for export goods. Indeed, the German government attempted to counteract the slump in demand in granting export subsidies worth two billion D-Mark and offering to

---

[109] See Rudolph, H. (1990), pp. 482-486.
[110] See Sachverständigenrat (1993), p. 375.
[111] See Koller, M. and T. Jung-Hammon (1993), p. 9.

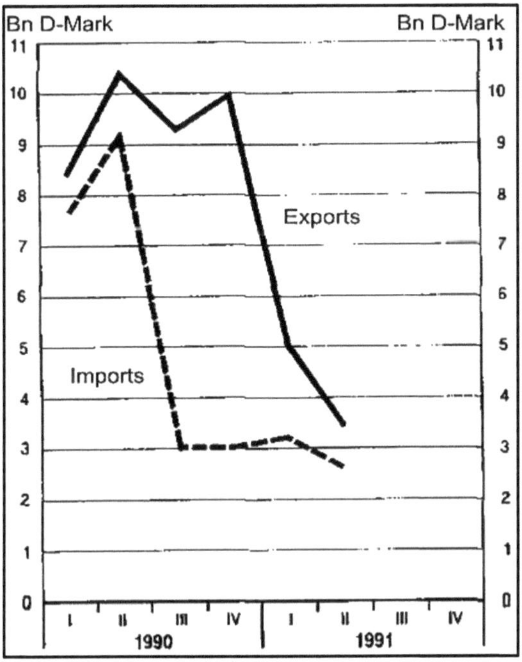

Notes: Inclusive of East Berlin; excludes trade with West Germany.

Figure 7: East German Foreign Trade, 1990-1991 [Sachverständigenrat (1991), p. 77, translated by the author.]

continue the account settlement in terms of transfer Roubles to former COMECON states.

However, as depicted in Figure 7, the success of these political measures was limited to a few months until December 1990, after which the dampening effect disappeared and exports to the COMECON states collapsed by close to 70 percent over the first two quarters of 1991.[112]

The interpretation of the suggested relation-ship between the calculated sector impact indicators and migration is intuitive: the higher the value of $impact_{k,i}$ for any sector k in sending district i, the higher emigration from that origin region. Correspondingly, in Figure 8 the total emigration volumes from each of the 35 EODs during 1991 and 1992 are plotted against the three individual sector push indicators. The illustration allows a comparison of the relationship between each sector impact and total migration to entire western Germany, represented by the left hand side plots, with the corresponding

[112] See Sachverständigenrat (1991), p. 77.

relationship in the surveyed sample of migration to the western metropolitan areas, depicted in the right hand side plots. The vertical axis denotes the total number of migrants in thousands and the value of the associated sector impact indicators are shown on the horizontal axis. A linear fit has been included to illustrate the prevailing positive relation between the shock impacts and emigration. A first glance at Figure 8 reveals that the calculated shock indicators, in particular the figures for the machinery manufacturing and electro-technical industry, are serving well in explaining the variation in total emigration across the EODs. Turning to the chemical industry, a positive but less clear relationship prevails which is likely due to factors arising from the specific character of this industrial segment: First, the production in the chemical sector of the former GDR was accompanied by a vast environmental pollution, which was further facilitated by the fact that the main industrial centres were, as discussed above, highly concentrated and commonly located nearby power and fuel production industrial hubs. In fact, the former GDR citizens were exposed to enormous environmental pollution and accompanied health risks. Overall, carbon dioxide emission in 1990 amounted to 18.6 tons per capita and year, ranking world's second highest after the USA with 20.8 tons, respective. In addition, sulphur dioxide emission in terms of area or inhabitants surmounted comparable figures across the globe, featuring emission values equal to ten times the magnitude of the FRG. The centres that showed the highest sulphur dioxide emission coincided with hubs of the chemical industry, concentrated in Saxony-Anhalt and adjacent parts of Saxony and Brandenburg.[113] Second, a large fraction of the chemical industry was located in the western part of the GDR, which gained increasing cen-

[113] See Perthes (1994), pp. 52-59.

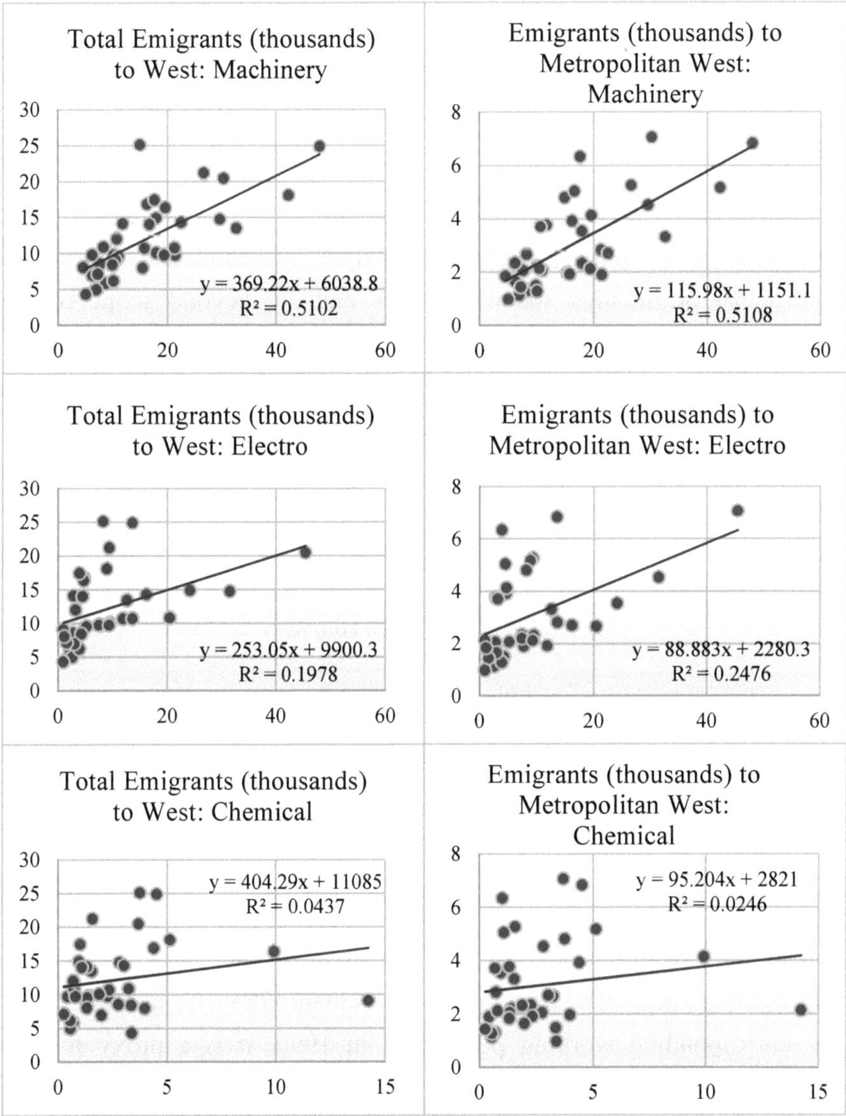

Figure 8: Sector Push vs Emigration (1991-'92) from 35 EODs [Adapted from German Federal Statistical Office (2014), Sachverständigenrat (1993), Koller, M. and T. Jung-Hammon (1993), Rudolph, H. (1990), data compilation.]

trality in the wake of reunification. Consequently, some of these areas, which are located close to the former inner German border may yield distortions to the sector specific pushing forces associated with the chemical industry, and hence, require special attention for the reasons discussed above.

Therefore, a preliminary regression analysis is conducted in order to control for origin area specific factors that are beyond scope of the sector-specific impacts' explanatory power in accounting for emigration. Accordingly, in order to predict exogenous migration, $\widehat{m}_{i,j,1991-92}$, the following regression model is estimated:

$$m_{i,j,1991-92} = \gamma_0 + \boldsymbol{\gamma_1} \frac{1}{D_{i,j}} \begin{pmatrix} impact_{machine,i} \\ impact_{electro,i} \\ impact_{chemical,i} \\ \frac{area_i}{working\ pop_{i,1990}} \times 1000 \end{pmatrix} \tag{VI}$$

$$+\omega_i + v_{i,j,1991-92} \,,$$

with $m_{i,j,1991-92}$ denoting cumulated actual migration from origin district i to metropolitan destination district j throughout 1991 and 1992. The vector of explanatory variables includes the calculated sector-specific impact indices and the ratio $\frac{area_i}{working\ pop_{i,1990}}$ as an additional measure of circuitousness of sending area i. The latter measure is expressed as the EODs' area in terms of square kilometre normalised by the corresponding working population in 1990. It is a proxy for the origin areas' relative agglomerative character, capturing the composition trade-off between urban and rural components. Intuitively, a relative large circuitousness ratio corresponds to a rural area, analogously, a low ratio indicates a highly agglomerated EOD. The agricultural sector was also negatively affected by unification, due to the formerly established *agricultural production cooperative (LPG)*, as it lacked efficiency on many counts.[114] Hence, a rural exodus was triggered and particularly remote locations experienced severe depopulation over the following decades.[115] Moreover, all explanatory variables are interacted with the inverted distance $D_{i,j}$ between each sending district i and recipient metropolitan area j, with $\boldsymbol{\gamma_1}$ denoting the corresponding vector of regression coefficients thereof. The distances between origin and recipient areas capture the relocation pattern of migration. That is, relatively distant destination regions are suggested to receive migrant inflows of lower magnitude in comparison to destinations which are located in close vicinity to migrants' origin areas.[116] Thus, since $D_{i,j}$ is suggested to be negatively related to migration and the vector of explanatory variables encompasses characteristics that are claimed to be positively related to migration, the distance variable is inverted to provide a measure for proximity, in order to avoid interaction distortions of the individual effects. In analogy to model equation (I), a border dummy variable ω_i is included to distinguish the EODs that are adjacent to the former zonal border from the remaining sending districts. The regression constant and the corresponding error term are denoted by γ_0 and $v_{i,j,1991-92}$. The descriptive statistics of the variables used to construct the instruments are provided in Table 4, depicting that the observed migrant streams comprise on average 42 people, whereas the difference between the largest and lowest flows is quite sizeable, amounting to 2,104 migrants. The proximity interacted sector shock index values indicate that the strongest pushing force arises on average from the machinery and vehicle construction sector while the lowest

114 See Rudolph, H. (1990), pp. 474-477.
115 See Sander, N. (2014), pp. 229-230.
116 See Ravenstein, E. G. (1885), p. 198.

	Obs	Mean	Std. Dev.	Min	Max
$m_{i,j,1991-92}$	2520	42.69841	98.39362	0	2104
$\frac{1}{D_{i,j}} \times impact_{machine,i}$	2520	.0535353	.0455525	.0077363	.6495075
$\frac{1}{D_{i,j}} \times impact_{electro,i}$	2520	.0291043	.0335543	.0017331	.3774212
$\frac{1}{D_{i,j}} \times impact_{chemical,i}$	2520	.0087413	.0108651	.0005741	.1008234
$\frac{1}{D_{i,j}} \frac{area_i}{working\ pop_{i,1990}} \times 1000$	2520	.0467175	.0368755	.0009121	.5010107

Note: Observations based on (35×72) =2520 pairwise combinations of origin and destination districts.

Table 4: Accounting for Migration (Descriptive Statistics) [Adapted from German Federal Statistical Office (2014), Sachverständigenrat (1993), Koller, M. and T. Jung-Hammon (1993), Rudolph, H. (1990), GeoHack (2014), data compilation.]

average migration hazard arises from the chemical industry, that is, $\frac{.0535353}{.0455525}(\approx 1.175) > \frac{.0291043}{.0335543}(\approx 0.867) > \frac{.0087413}{.0108651}(\approx 0.805)$. As afore mentioned, the relative concentration of the sectors in specific East German production hubs, which are either proximate to or further apart from West Germany and/or located in the border area districts, may play an important role in explaining the degree of the pushing forces. Moreover, the average push generated by proximity interacted circuitousness is on average the strongest among the explanatory variables, that is, $\frac{.0467175}{.0368755}(\approx 1.267)$. Intuitively, a rising value of this interaction term accounts for an increase in the propensity to migrate, arising from either a comparably larger area per capita (precisely per working population in 1990) at a given proximity to the West, or a district that is relatively closer situated at a given areal unit per capita, or a combination thereof.

The corresponding OLS regression results of model equation (VI) are attainable in Table 5. Specifications (1) to (3) show the coefficient estimates of the explanatory variables if the border area dummies are included. All variables apart from the proximity interacted impact of the chemical sector are significant in explaining emigration from the 35 EODs. Moreover, dropping the latter variable in specification (2) and moreover dropping the proximity interacted impact of the electronics industry (3) slightly reduces the overall model fit, denoted by R^2, whereas the remaining coefficients pertain significance in line with a reduction in the respective standard errors, shown in parentheses. However, if the border dummy variable is excluded, solely the effect of proximity interacted circuitousness as well as the shock impact of the machinery construction industry retain significant explanatory power of the observed emigrant outflows. The corresponding coefficient estimates of the model specifications excluding border dummies are denoted in column (4) to (6). Furthermore, the estimated constant term of the model is significant in all six specification and the *F*-statistics' *p*-value for the joint significance of all coefficient estimates is p =0.0000 throughout model specifications (1) to (6). The overall association between the dependent variable and all explanatory variables is strongest in specification (1), displaying an R^2 of 0.120.

Based on the acquired coefficient estimates of model (VI) the predicted migration values $\widehat{m}_{i,j,1991-92,spec}$ for specifications (1) to (6) are obtained, where the added index $spec$ denotes the respective specification.

Table 5: Accounting for Migration (Regression Results)

	(1) Migration 1991-'92	(2) Migration 1991-'92	(3) Migration 1991-'92	(4) Migration 1991-'92	(5) Migration 1991-'92	(6) Migration 1991-'92
$\frac{1}{D_{i,j}} \times impact_{machine,i}$	539.5***	521.9***	589.7***	560.9***	543.6***	571.1***
	(54.49)	(51.12)	(40.99)	(54.57)	(51.17)	(40.94)
$\frac{1}{D_{i,j}} \times impact_{electro,i}$	151.3**	157.9**		55.15	61.71	
	(71.61)	(71.25)		(69.27)	(68.90)	
$\frac{1}{D_{i,j}} \times impact_{chemical,i}$	-171.5			-168.9		
	(183.7)			(184.5)		
$\frac{1}{D_{i,j}} \times \frac{area_i}{working\ pop_{i,1990}} \times 1000$	536.1***	533.0***	512.9***	462.8***	459.8***	455.1***
	(52.82)	(52.71)	(51.96)	(50.96)	(50.85)	(50.57)
Constant	-7.433**	-8.043**	-6.944*	-9.082**	-9.681***	-9.134***
	(3.644)	(3.585)	(3.553)	(3.646)	(3.586)	(3.534)
Border DV	Yes	Yes	Yes	No	No	No
Observations	2520	2520	2520	2520	2520	2520
Origin areas	35	35	35	35	35	35
R^2	0.120	0.119	0.118	0.111	0.111	0.110

Notes: 1. Standard errors in parentheses.
2. Significance levels: * $p < 0.10$, ** $p < 0.05$, *** $p < 0.01$.
3. Observations are (35×72) =2520 pairwise combinations of origin and destination districts.

[Author's representation adapted from German Federal Statistical Office (2014), Sachverständigenrat (1993), Koller, M. and T. Jung-Hammon (1993), Rudolph, Helmut (1990), GeoHack (2014), data compilation.]

The correlation matrix of each predicted variable $\widehat{m}_{i,j,1991-92,spec}$ with the actual migration variable $m_{i,j,1991-92}$ is displayed below:

$$corr\left(m_{i,j,1991-92}, \widehat{m}_{i,j,1991-92,spec}\right) = \qquad \text{(VII)}$$

$$\begin{pmatrix} 1 & & & & & & \\ 0.3460 & 1 & & & & & \\ 0.3456 & 0.99 & 1 & & & & \\ 0.3431 & 0.99 & 0.99 & 1 & & & \\ 0.3333 & 0.96 & 0.96 & 0.96 & 1 & & \\ 0.3456 & 0.99 & 1 & 0.99 & 0.96 & 1 & \\ 0.3431 & 0.99 & 0.99 & 1 & 0.96 & 0.99 & 1 \end{pmatrix}.$$

It prevails that the correlations do not vary by much across the specifications, however, specification (1) of model (VI) is chosen for the instrumental variable construction as the inferred predicted migration $\widehat{m}_{i,j,1991-92,(1)}$ exhibits the strongest correlation, that is 0.346, as well as the best overall model fit among all specifications. Moreover, the corresponding adjusted R^2 of regression specification (1) is 0.118 and the F-statistic for the joint significance of all variables is 68.38 with a corresponding p-value of 0.0000, as mentioned above.

Notably, since model (VI) rests upon a theory of origin specific push factors of migration, the predicted values of migration are linear combinations of factors that are exogenous to migrants' destination areas. As argued and practised by several scholars, no standard error correction is necessary in applying a generated instrument, which is a function of estimated parameters, to a standard two-stage least squares procedure.[117]

Furthermore, the purpose of this procedure is to generate the required instrumental variable for immigration to the 72 urban districts, presented

[117] See Wooldridge, J. M. (2010), pp. 116-117; Frank, D. (2009), p. 9.

in model (I); however, $m_{j,1991-92}$ and the variable $\widehat{m}_{i,j,1991-92,(1)}$ feature different levels of aggregation. Thus, redefining predicted migration from origin i to destination j:

$$\hat{z}_{i,j,1991-92} = \widehat{m}_{i,j,1991-92,(1)}, \tag{VIII}$$

moreover, adding the corresponding 35 individually estimated migrant inflows per metropolitan area:

$$\hat{z}_{j,1991-92} = \sum_i \hat{z}_{i,j,1991-92}, \tag{IX}$$

yields the forecasted number of immigrants for each of the 72 urban districts. That is, the instrumental variable $\hat{z}_{j,1991-92}$, introduced in Section 3.1. For completeness, replacing $\widehat{m}_{i,j,1991-92,(1)}$ by $\widehat{m}_{i,j,1991-92,spec}$ in equation (VIII) and $\hat{z}_{i,j,1991-92}$ by $\hat{z}_{i,j,1991-92,spec}$ in equation (VIII) and (IX), the correlation matrix of actual aggregated migration $m_{j,1991-92}$ and the created instruments for each of the six introduced specifications is provided below:

$$corr\left(m_{j,1991-92}, \hat{z}_{j,1991-92,spec}\right) = \tag{X}$$

$$\begin{pmatrix} 1 & & & & & & \\ 0.6261 & 1 & & & & & \\ 0.6254 & 1 & 1 & & & & \\ 0.6221 & 0.99 & 0.99 & 1 & & & \\ 0.6252 & 1 & 1 & 0.99 & 1 & & \\ 0.6254 & 1 & 1 & 0.99 & 1 & 1 & \\ 0.6221 & 0.99 & 0.99 & 1 & 0.99 & 0.99 & 1 \end{pmatrix}.$$

Accordingly, the choice of specification (1) to create the desired instrument is further supported, based on the fact that it moreover yields a correlation coefficient with the endogenous explanatory variable of the main regression model of 0.6261, which is the highest among the six specifications of model (VI). The created instrument for observed migration $m_{j,1991-92}$ will be applied to model (I) in a standard two-stage least squares procedure in Section 4.2 of the subsequent chapter.

4 Results

The present chapter serves to report the regression results for the model presented in Section 3.1. The baseline results of the OLS estimation are presented in Section 4.1, followed by a summary of the parallel results employing an instrumental variable estimation, which is provided in Section 4.2. The chapter concludes with a discussion of inferred implications in Section 4.3.

4.1 OLS Estimation

In order to estimate the marginal effects of immigration on changes in rental prices, a standard Ordinary Least Squares procedure is applied to model (I). As discussed in the previous chapter, the respective results are potentially biased due to problems associated with the endogeneity of the main explanatory variable. Accordingly, the regression results essentially provide a baseline for a comparison with the instrumental variable estimation results presented in the subsequent section.

With reference to Section 3.1, the reported marginal effects on the dependent variables $\Delta \log(rent_{j,c,1990-92})$, with $c \in \{minimum, average, maximum\}$, denote the percent change in primary letting prices of rental category c, per percent increase in the housing markets' population due to East German immigration. In the proceedings of the study the marginal effects will be shortly referred to as 'a x percent change in rental or letting prices due to a one percent migration impact'.

The descriptive statistics of the variables used in the analysis are provided in Table 6, indicating that the first-differences in the outcome variable $\Delta \log(rent_{j,min,1990-92})$ range from 0 to 0.176, which corre-

	Obs	Mean	Std. Dev.	Min	Max
Δ Log rent minimum	72	.0749038	.0386303	0	.1760913
Δ Log rent average	72	.0679738	.0272086	.019641	.1522128
Δ Log rent maximum	72	.0634117	.0350843	0	.1763745
(Immigrants 1991-'92) / (Population '90)	72	.0061475	.003342	.0013453	.0234371
(Arrivals '90)/ (Population '90)	72	1.125823	.8708429	.0835448	4.320887
Unemployment rate '90	72	.0898194	.0297427	.04	.156
Arrivals trend	72	.0065348	.034287	-.0843751	.109174

Table 6: Main Regression (Descriptive Statistics) [Author's representation adapted from bulwiengesa AG, RIWIS (2014a) and German Federal Statistical Office (2014), data compilation.]

sponds to a range in rental price changes between 0 and 50 percent from 1990 to 1992, and moreover an outstanding average change of approximately 18.8 percent. Analogously, the observed differences in log average and maximum rents show an approximate range from 0.02 to 0.15 and 0 to 0.18, respectively. The equivalent percentage change values amount to 4.63 to 41.98 and 0 to 50.1. Accordingly, the observed price rise for the two outcome categories equals on average 17.17 and 16.1 percent. Turning to the explanatory variables, the cumulative immigration treatment to the 72 metropolitan areas throughout 1991 and 1992 represented on average 0.61 percent of the initial population in 1990, ranging from 0.13 to 2.34 percent. Moreover, the lowest unemployment rate among the 72 cities equalled four percent, while the highest rate marked 15.6 percent, well above the observed average of 8.98 percent. Hence, controlling for unemployment appears to be reasonable in the underlying sample. Last, with reference to Section 3.1 the tourism control variables comprise index values for attractiveness and the adequate trend development at the onset of migration. More precisely, the values range from 0.084 to 4.321 tourists per capita, out of which the observed cities received on average 1.13 visitors per inhabitant in 1990. Moreover, the appendant trend development figures range from -0.08 to 0.11, whereat positive values represent upbeat areas and negative values indicate declining attractiveness.

The marginal effects on this vast development in rental prices, which can be attributed to migration, are summarised in Tables 7 to 9, depicting the regression results for the three outcomes. The immigration impact on rental prices varies across the specified outcomes. Table 7 shows a consistently significant impact of immigration on the minimum level rental prices of primary let flats across all six specifications of model (I). Precisely, the first column denotes a highly statistically significant impact of migration at the one percent level: a one percent population increase in the cities' housing markets due to East German immigration is suggested to yield an increase in the minimum category of rental prices by 4.831 percent. Specification (1) is based on a regression of the rental outcome on solely the main explanatory variable of interest, in which the corresponding constant term estimate of 0.0554 is also significant at the one percent level. Moreover, adding controls alters the magnitude of the coefficient estimates within a range of −1.2 to +0.9 percentage points: Controlling for time-invariant characteristics in specification (2) reduces the magnitude of the coefficient estimate to 3.6 percent at the five percent significance level. Prevailingly, the tourism variable *arrivals per initial population* seems to be the only robust control correlate of rental price changes across specifications and investigated rental outcomes. Accordingly, the coefficient estimate in specification (2) suggests a highly significant positive impact of amenities on rental prices. That is, an increase in the cities' attractive-

	(1) Δ Log rent	(2) Δ Log rent	(3) Δ Log rent	(4) Δ Log rent	(5) Δ Log rent	(6) Δ Log rent
(Immigrants 1991-'92) / (Pop. '90)	4.831*** (1.784)	3.608** (1.795)	5.479** (2.259)	4.471*** (1.676)	4.811* (2.585)	5.768** (2.449)
(Arrivals '90) / (Pop. '90)		0.0283*** (0.00705)				0.0196*** (0.00493)
Unemployment rate '90		0.250 (0.211)				0.115 (0.233)
Arrivals trend		0.125 (0.167)				-0.0589 (0.122)
Constant	0.0554*** (0.0120)	0.00470 (0.0273)	0.0529*** (0.0124)	0.0418*** (0.0118)	0.0338* (0.0194)	-0.0129 (0.0406)
Border dummy	No	No	Yes	No	No	Yes
Market type dummies	No	No	No	Yes	No	Yes
State dummies	No	No	No	No	Yes	Yes
Observations	72	72	72	72	72	72
R^2	0.096	0.310	0.102	0.392	0.496	0.648

Notes: 1. Heteroskedasticity robust standard errors in parentheses.
2. Significance: $^{*}\ p < 0.10$, $^{**}\ p < 0.05$, $^{***}\ p < 0.01$
3. All regressions are weighted by initial population.

Table 7: Ordinary Least Squares - Minimum Rents (primary let) [Author's representation adapted from bulwiengesa AG, RIWIS (2014a) and German Federal Statistical Office (2014), data compilation.]

ness, expressed in an additional annual visit per capita, yields a rental price increase by about 0.03 percent. The estimated coefficients of the unemployment rate are positive yet insignificant in specification (2) and (7); whereas the corresponding estimated marginal effect of the arrivals trend indicator is positive in specification (2) while negative in (7), however, both estimates are insignificant. In specifications (3) through (6) dummy variables are added. The consideration of the border dummy increases the migration impact on rents to 5.479 percent; however, the standard errors increase as well and the significance level is slightly reduced. Compared to specification (1), employing state level controls in specification (5) does not change the magnitude of the estimated marginal effect of immigration by much; however, the associated standard error increases from 1.784 to 2.585, thus, reducing the significance level to ten percent. In contrast, controlling for market type yields a reduction in the estimated marginal migration impact as well as the standard error by 0.36 and 0.11 percentage points, respectively. Accordingly, the estimated impact in specification (4) is also highly significant at the one percent level. Simultaneously, the overall model fit improved substantially featuring an R^2 of 0.392, as opposed to the R^2 of specification (1), which equals 0.096. Finally, specification (6) suggests a 5.768 percent increase in rental prices due to a one percent migration impact if all controls are jointly applied. The estimate is statistically significant at the five percent level, and notably, the degree of association between all explanatory variables and the rental outcome is at roughly 65 percent, the highest among all specifications and investigated rental categories.

Prior to the discussion of the pertinent results of the average and maximum level rental categories it is worth noting that heteroskedasticity robust standard errors are reported and referred to in all regression tables and related argumentation. The provision of heteroskedasticity robust standard errors follows from a consideration of the *Breusch-Pagan / Cook-Weisberg* test for heteroskedasticity. That is, a test on the residuals is run under the assumption that homoskedasticity held. Precisely, if the null hypothesis that the residuals exhibit constant variances cannot be rejected, heteroskedasticity should not pose a problem. For instance, considering regression specification (1) for the minimum category rental outcome discussed above, the test is conducted under the null hypothesis:

$$H_0: var(\varepsilon_{j,1990-92}|m_{j,1991-92}) = \sigma^2. \tag{XI}$$

The resulting F-statistic yields $F(1,70)=18.28$ with a corresponding p-value of 0.0001. Consequently, as the p-value is significantly small the null hypothesis of homoskedasticity is rejected.[118]

Turning to Table 8, the regression results for the average rental price category of primary lets furthermore suggest a consistently significant positive impact of migration on the change in rents, apart from specification (5), which depicts a positive yet insignificant coefficient estimate. The results of this outcome variable are of particular interest to the analysis at hand, as the commensurate average rental values replicate the development of the entire West German housing market to the largest part. Accordingly, specification (1) implies a 3.328 percent increase in average rents due to East German immigration equal to one percent of the initial population. Thus, the estimated effect is 1.503 percentage points lower than its minimum rental category counterpart. However, the related degree of association between the explanatory and dependent variable, denoted by R^2, has slightly improved to 0.108 and the significance level of both, the marginal effect of migration as well as the constant term, is marked at the one percent level. Adding time-variant controls in specification (2) and additionally the full set of dummies in specification (6) reduces the estimated marginal migration impact by 0.69 and 0.23 percentage points and moreover results in lower significance levels of five and ten percent, respectively. In addition, controlling for border area location across metropolitan areas yields a highly significant increase of the estimated change in rents to roughly four percent per one percent immigration treatment. Notwithstanding,

---

[118] See Wooldridge, J. M. (2013), pp. 265-267.

	(1) Δ Log rent	(2) Δ Log rent	(3) Δ Log rent	(4) Δ Log rent	(5) Δ Log rent	(6) Δ Log rent
(Immigrants 1991-'92) / (Pop. '90)	3.328*** (1.127)	2.638** (1.079)	4.005*** (1.485)	3.241*** (1.161)	1.779 (1.749)	3.098* (1.792)
(Arrivals '90) / (Pop. '90)		0.0158*** (0.00477)				0.0113** (0.00471)
Unemployment rate '90		0.135 (0.109)				-0.0489 (0.159)
Arrivals trend		-0.0641 (0.118)				-0.0898 (0.121)
Constant	0.0534*** (0.00749)	0.0264* (0.0146)	0.0508*** (0.00811)	0.0389*** (0.00803)	0.0466** (0.0181)	0.0378 (0.0282)
Border dummy	No	No	Yes	No	No	Yes
Market type dummies	No	No	No	Yes	No	Yes
State dummies	No	No	No	No	Yes	Yes
Observations	72	72	72	72	72	72
R^2	0.108	0.326	0.123	0.244	0.384	0.535

Notes: 1. Heteroskedasticity robust standard errors in parentheses.
2. Significance: $^{*}\ p < 0.10$, $^{**}\ p < 0.05$, $^{***}\ p < 0.01$
3. All regressions are weighted by initial population.

Table 8: Ordinary Least Squares - Average Rents (primary let) [Author's representation adapted from bulwiengesa AG, RIWIS (2014a) and German Federal Statistical Office (2014), data compilation.]

the inclusion of market type dummies in specification (4) yields a fairly robust and highly significant result in comparison to the marginal effect determined by means of specification (1).

Altogether, compared to the minimum category rental outcome, the reported regression coefficients applicable to average rents are relatively smaller in magnitude. Nevertheless, the propounded migration impact is still sizeable and the main reason for the presence of a reduced effect may stem from the relative rigidity of the observed upper bound rents in the present analysis. Intuitively, the impact of the analysed East-West migration is presumably low, since the vast majority of migrants arrived with relatively poor financial endowment alongside precarious employment prospects, thence, targeting the lower bound to mid-level rental categories. Consequently, the migration induced increase in demand for flats in the upper bound market segment was conceivably low.

The latter effect is likewise replicated in the corresponding results for the OLS regressions of the maximum rental price category of primary let dwellings on immigration. Thence, focusing on the summarised outcome in Table 9, it becomes apparent that there is no clear association between immigration and the development in the upper level rental segment. The baseline specification as well as specifications (2) and (4) yield a comparably low and insignificant estimated marginal effect of immigration on rents. Controlling for state affiliation yields an estimated coefficient of 3.773 at the ten percent significance level, which is fairly similar in magnitude to the average rental category results. Likewise, from the inclusion of the border dummy variable follows an impact of immigration that is in line with the reported marginal effects in the minimum rental category and significant at the five percent level. Finally, specification (6) yields a coefficient estimate of 6.05 at the five percent level, which is the largest suggested marginal effect of immigration as of yet. Nevertheless, the results for the maximum rental category are imprecise and highly volatile. In addition, the overall model fit is comparably low across all six specifications, ranging from 0.052 to 0.285.

Notably, all regressions of the West German housing market outcomes presented in this thesis are weighted by initial population in 1990. From

	(1) Δ Log rent	(2) Δ Log rent	(3) Δ Log rent	(4) Δ Log rent	(5) Δ Log rent	(6) Δ Log rent
(Immigrants 1991-'92) / (Pop. '90)	2.753 (1.774)	2.716 (1.913)	4.031** (1.952)	2.766 (1.813)	3.773* (2.232)	6.050** (2.358)
(Arrivals '90) / (Pop. '90)		0.0111* (0.00649)				0.00881 (0.00889)
Unemployment rate '90		0.231 (0.161)				0.403* (0.233)
Arrivals trend		0.214 (0.146)				0.193 (0.162)
Constant	0.0509*** (0.0123)	0.0150 (0.0203)	0.0461*** (0.0130)	0.0432*** (0.0112)	0.0281 (0.0212)	-0.0140 (0.0409)
Border dummy	No	No	Yes	No	No	Yes
Market type dummies	No	No	No	Yes	No	Yes
State dummies	No	No	No	No	Yes	Yes
Observations	72	72	72	72	72	72
R^2	0.052	0.125	0.091	0.069	0.172	0.285

Notes: 1. Heteroskedasticity robust standard errors in parentheses.
2. Significance: * $p < 0.10$, ** $p < 0.05$, *** $p < 0.01$
3. All regressions are weighted by initial population.

Table 9: Ordinary Least Squares - Maximum Rents (primary let) [Author's representation adapted from bulwiengesa AG, RIWIS (2014a) and German Federal Statistical Office (2014), data compilation.]

a research perspective it may be interesting to treat all 72 investigative units equally, neglecting population weights. However, from a political point of view, the application of weighted regressions appears to be more reasonable.[119] This is due to the fact that the weights attribute relatively more importance to the immigration impact in housing markets of comparably larger cities in which more people are affected by the correspondent rental price development. Moreover, investigating the rate

119 See Saiz, A. (2007), p. 355.

of change in letting prices from one point in time to another, the observed rental level prior to the introduction of the treatment is crucial. That is, given conventional property market conditions, the initial rental level in 1990 features presumably lower values in relatively small metropolitan areas than in larger cities. This is a generally observed phenomenon that stems from a variety of economic factors, such as income level differences between lager and smaller cities, as well as differing demand and supply conditions. Hypothetically, an equal letting price increase in absolute terms will accordingly be expressed in a comparably larger percentage increase in housing markets, which featured lower initial property values. This effect may be of particular relevance in the present analysis, due to the large variations in the surveyed urban districts' size in terms of population. Accordingly, in Figure 9, the initial rental level values prior to the application of the migration treatment is plotted against each cities' population in 1990. For illustrative purposes, the variables are centred at the respective sample mean. Prevalent is a positive relation between the size of the surveyed urban districts and the initial rental prices. That is, an above average populated city is characterised by above average rents and vice versa; however, with some exceptions. Data points in the upper left quadrant depict metropolitan areas with a relative low population featuring above average rental prices. Potential candidates in this segment are relatively small urban locations that benefit from specific amenities. On the contrary, some outliers in the lower right-hand-side quadrant represent relatively large cities with below average letting prices. Unfavourable factors, such as the former zonal border area location, are potential driving forces of this segment, as discussed in Section 3. Accordingly, if larger increases in rents are systematically observed among the smaller investigative units, those impacts will be overrepresented if regressions are not weighted by affected population. Thus, the overall result will likely be upward biased and not representative of the average housing market development if the intension is to consider welfare effects of immigration on the native population.

Moreover, throughout the empirical work conducted for the purpose of this thesis, additional regressions have been run for rental outcomes of

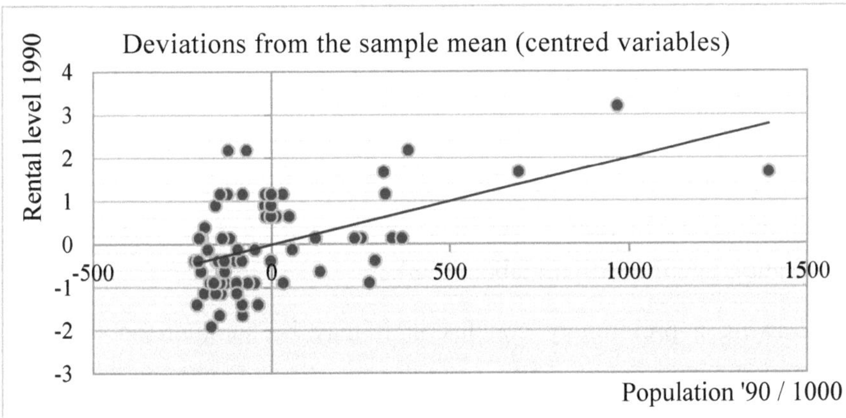

Figure 9: Initial Rental Level vs Population [Author's representation adapted from bulwiengesa AG, RIWIS (2014a), dataset.]

secondary let flats. However, the results have been inconclusive, which was initially not anticipated, since the corresponding average annual rates of change, depicted in Figure 6 in Section 3.2.3, were substantially higher than the primary let counterparts. Accordingly, additional regressions were run based on the change in rental values deferred by an additional year, that is, the change from 1991 to 1993 instead of 1990 to 1992. The outcomes thereof showed better overall model fits and were more precise, yet estimates were hardly significant. Hence, the improvement of the results employing the modified lag structure lends some support to the previously discussed argument that secondary rental prices adjust less quickly to shifts in demand than those of primary lets. However, the distortions may eminently also be simply due to the fact that the present sample size is unfortunately very small and the observed time span rather limited, amongst others.

Finally, the effect of immigration on property purchasing prices has been studied. However, no meaningful association has been determined. Intuitively, this result is plausible on the grounds of the financial constraints of the East German immigrants and the challenges they have encountered with regards to their integration in the local labour markets. Much of the observed German internal migration occurred spontaneous with little prior financial planning or preparation and particularly the accreditation of and demand for workers who formerly acquired GDR professional qualifications posed several challenges to a successful integration into the western labour market.[120]

In drawing a preliminary conclusion it may be summarised that the regression results largely vary across the investigated rental categories as well as the individual specifications therein. Particularly, the findings for the upper level rental category are inconclusive, which is likely due to the reasons discussed above. However, the results become more clear when focusing on the mid to low level housing market segment. Specifically the investigation of the minimum rental category provided evidence of a statistically significant impact of German internal migration on the West German housing market: a one percent increase in the housing market's population due to immigration yields an increase in minimum level rents of primary let dwellings by approximately five percent. Analogously, the study of the mid-level market segment suggests a three to five percent increase in average rents of primary let

[120] See Troltsch, K. (1993), pp. 63-66.

dwellings due to a one percent migration impact. The underlying results are three to five times larger in magnitude than the homologous findings by Albert Saiz in 2007,[121] and if compared to the results of Stillman and Mare in 2008,[122] likewise Kalantaryan, Sona in 2013,[123] the difference in the estimated effect is far more sizeable. In order to attain an overview of whether the discussed outcomes change when the instrumental variable is applied, the corresponding results from the 2SLS regressions are presented in the following section.

121 See Saiz, A. (2007), p. 354.
122 See Stillman, S. and D. C. Maré (2008), pp. 17-19 and appendix table 7-8.
123 See Kalantaryan, S. (2013), pp. 21-22.

4.2 IV Estimation

Departing from the discussion of the OLS results, this section turns to the application of the dedicated instrumental variable estimation technique to the three investigated rental price outcomes. Table 10 depicts the first stage regression estimates of the 2SLS procedure. In the first stage the endogenous explanatory variable $m_{j,1991-92}$, that is, actual immigration received by the 72 metropolitan areas divided by initial population, is regressed on the generated instrument of predicted immigration $\hat{z}_{j,1991-92}$ as well as the remaining control variables of the main regression model (I). Specifications (1) through (6) are the accordant specifications presented in the discussion of the OLS results. Hence, the resulting coefficient estimates show that the constructed instrument is highly significant in the presented settings, apart from specification (6); which nevertheless, shows a relatively high *t*-statistic and a corresponding *p*-value of 0.11. Moreover, the associated critical value of the *F*-test for the excluded instrument is very high, lending additional support to the exploitation of the IV in the analysis at hand. Analogously, the first five specifications feature relatively high *t*-statistics as well as *F*-test critical values for the excluded instrument that are consistently above ten, indicating that predicted immigration based on origin characteristics constitutes a well-defined IV for $m_{j,1991-92}$.

At a first glance it may seem unclear why the present study exploits an IV of predicted immigration for actual immigration divided by the destinations' initial population, instead of an instrument of predicted immigration that is analogously divided by initial population. The answer results from the fact that initial population of destination *j* poses an endogenous factor in the given analysis of rental prices. Likewise, a city which is characterised by a relatively large population among the

Table 10: First Stage Regressions

	(1)	(2)	(3)	(4)	(5)	(6)
	$m_{j,1991-92}$	$m_{j,1991-92}$	$m_{j,1991-92}$	$m_{j,1991-92}$	$m_{j,1991-92}$	$m_{j,1991-92}$
$\hat{z}_{j,1991-92}$	2.89e-06***	3.16e-06***	2.32e-06***	2.92e-06***	1.98e-06**	1.57e-06
	(5.44)	(7.08)	(3.94)	(5.49)	(2.51)	(1.62)
Time variant-controls	No	Yes	No	No	No	Yes
Border DV	No	No	Yes	No	No	Yes
Market type dummies	No	No	No	Yes	No	Yes
State dummies	No	No	No	No	Yes	Yes
Observations	72	72	72	72	72	72
R^2	0.34	0.50	0.36	0.35	0.71	0.75
F excluded instrument	29.56	16.29	21.37	10.57	47.68	71.43

Notes: 1. t-statistics in parentheses.
2. Significance: * $p < 0.10$, ** $p < 0.05$, *** $p < 0.01$
3. All regressions are weighted by initial population.

[Author's representation adapted from bulwiengesa AG, RIWIS (2014a), German Federal Statistical Office (2014), Sachverständigenrat (1993), Koller, M. and T. Jung-Hammon (1993), Rudolph, H. (1990), data compilation.]

surveyed destination areas exhibits a stronger pull effect on migrants to the area. Since the underlying instrumentation technique employs a theory that rests entirely on push factors associated with origin area characteristics, the considered destination pull is an effect the created instrument of predicted migration simply cannot account for. Thence, the predicted values of exogenous migration consistently underestimate actual migrant streams to large cities and in aggregating the detailed estimates the deviations from the true observations further increase. However, those deviations are in fact the reason why the instrument is constructed in the first place, as the purpose is to separate the endogenous from the exogenous component of migration and exploit exclusively the latter in the preceding analysis. In some respect, the main explanatory variable of model (I), per definition, already corrects for the described pull effect in normalising immigration by initial population. Thus, further dividing $\hat{z}_{j,1991-92}$ by initial population would yield an instrument, which first, includes an endogenous component, and second, features an association with $m_{j,1991-92}$ that predominantly arises from the variations in population among observations, as opposed to the covariation between actual and predicted migration. Both of the above characteristics are pertinent arguments against the division of the instrumental variable by the destination areas' initial population.

A final note on the quality of the constructed instrument relates to the justification of the exogeneity assumption thereof. In Section 3.2.4 sufficient exogeneity has been solely inferred from a factual argumentation that the origin based driving forces of emigration were plausibly unrelated to the housing market outcomes in the West. Unfortunately, the fact that the number of instruments equals the number of endogenous explanatory variables in the given setting prevents to employ a test of this exogeneity assumption. Noteworthy, the preparation of this thesis further involved the construction of two individual IVs that were jointly applied in the 2SLS estimation, for which a test of overidentifying restrictions may be applied. Namely, the first instrument is derived from a combination of the three individual sector shocks interacted with the proximity effect, that is,

$$\frac{1}{D_{i,j}} \times \left(impact_{machine,i} + impact_{electro,i} + impact_{chemical,i}\right), \quad \text{(XII)}$$

and the second instrument is constructed from the proximity interacted circuitousness effect, $\frac{1}{D_{i,j}} \times \frac{area_i}{working\ pop_{i,1990}} \times 1000$, specified in Section 3.2.4. The attained values from (XII) are added across origin regions for each destination and the second instrument is constructed by calculating the mean value of the corresponding 35 circuitousness variable values for each destination city. Further results of this instrumentation variant have been omitted from this thesis, as they lack in several aspects behind the preferred instrument $\hat{z}_{j,1991-92}$. Nonetheless, since the two individual IVs are constructed using the same information as the preliminary regressions in predicting migration, it may be informative to report the results of Sargan's test for overidentifying restrictions at this stage. More precisely, due to the presence of heteroskedastic error terms the Wooldridge test, an adaptation of the Sargan test, has been conducted under the null hypothesis that the instruments are valid. For instance, the respective test from the 2SLS (unweight) regression of specification (1) for the minimum rental category yields a χ^2- distributed test score of 0.000483 and a corresponding *p*-value equal to 0.9825. Thus, the null on the validity of the separate IVs is not rejected on the grounds of the highly insignificant *p*-value.[124] Since the presented test provides

[124] See Cameron, A. C. and P. K. Trivedi (2009), p. 277; Wooldridge, J. M. (2013), pp. 515-516.

evidence of the exogeneity of the two separate instruments, the validity of $\hat{z}_{j,1991-92}$ is further supported as its construction relies essentially on the same information.

Turning to the results of the IV regression, Table 11 summarises the coefficient estimates from the second stage regression of the 2SLS procedure. In the second stage fitted values from the first stage regressions are employed. The results are less concise than the corresponding OLS estimates and deviate largely from the baseline results across specifications and rental outcomes. Specifically, the IV regressions for the minimum rents report inconclusive estimates of the marginal effect of immigration on the change in letting prices. That is, specifications (3), (5) and (6) produced relatively consistent and statistically significant estimates in the OLS application; however, in using the IV the coefficient estimates substantially, yet insignificantly, over- or understate the effects. It further prevails that specification (5) even suggests a negative marginal effect of immigration on minimum and average rents, of respective −1.749 and −3.622. Nevertheless, these results are statistically insignificant; whereas, those estimates that are significant at the ten, five or one percent level, across outcomes and specifications, are much larger in magnitude than their OLS counterparts. Some of the regressions suggest rental price elasticities that are almost double in magnitude of the corresponding OLS results. Indeed, the coefficient estimates are on average approximately 50 percentage points larger across the minimum and average rental categories, while the third specification of the change in maximum rents yields a significant estimate at the five percent level that is roughly double the magnitude of the related OLS coefficient. Interestingly, the analysed average rental category produces the most concise and robust results, which is arguably the most representative measure of the West

	Coefficients Reported: (Immigrants 1991-'92) / (Population '90)					
Dependent Variable	(1)	(2)	(3)	(4)	(5)	(6)
Δ Log rent (minimum)	7.950* (4.192)	6.912** (3.395)	13.18 (8.422)	6.737*** (2.230)	-1.749 (4.769)	1.184 (7.525)
Δ Log rent (average)	4.089* (2.179)	4.119** (1.780)	7.121* (4.124)	3.929** (1.786)	-3.622 (4.037)	4.119** (1.780)
Δ Log rent (maximum)	3.383 (2.829)	1.832 (2.816)	8.324** (4.204)	3.228 (2.943)	0.810 (5.469)	1.832 (2.816)
Border dummy	No	No	Yes	No	No	Yes
Market type dummies	No	No	No	Yes	No	Yes
State dummies	No	No	No	No	Yes	Yes
Observations	72	72	72	72	72	72

Notes: 1. Heteroskedasticity robust standard errors in parentheses.
2. Significance: * $p < 0.10$, ** $p < 0.05$, *** $p < 0.01$
3. All regressions are weighted by initial population.

Table 11: IV Regression Results - Minimum, Average and Maximum Rents (primary let) [Author's representation adapted from bulwiengesa AG, RIWIS (2014a) and German Federal Statistical Office (2014), data compilation.]

German property market among the three endogenous variables studied. Moreover, the astonishing jump in estimated impacts of the minimum rental category provides support of the argument that migrants tend to settle where rental prices grow at a relatively lower rate, causing a downward bias in the related OLS estimates.

On the one hand, the deviations among the OLS and IV coefficients suggest that the OLS results of the presented analysis are downward biased. On the other hand, due to the very restricted sample surveyed in the present analysis, the instrumental variable coefficient estimates are potentially also severely biased.[125] Nonetheless, the analysis at hand provides a first indication of an empirically evident impact of immigration on rental prices in destination housing markets. Thus, further research endeavours may involve the study of the underlying concepts in exploring an extended sample, which is however, beyond the scope of this master thesis.

In spite of the limitations of the presented analysis, the results from the 2SLS analysis suggest that an immigration inflow equal to one percent of the initial population triggered a rental price growth of on average 5.47 percent in West German housing markets. The average refers to all statistically significant coefficient estimates, while the effects range across rental categories and differing specifications of model (I), between 3.929 and 8.324 percent. To allow a comparison with the main OLS results outlined in section 4.1 the observed effect on the minimum rental category shows that an immigrant inflow equal to one percent of the initial population is associated with an increase in minimum rents of roughly seven percent, as opposed to an average fivc percent increase, reported in the OLS regressions. In addition, the estimated impact on average rental prices amounts to roughly 4.7 as opposed to 3.3 percent depicted in the OLS procedure. Unsurprisingly, the results of the top end market segment are fairly inconclusive, which is likely due to a presumable modest increase in demand for those relatively expensive rental units, associated with the underlying case of German East-West migration.

[125] See Wooldridge, J. M. (2013), p. 495.

4.3 Implications

The results of the given empirical investigation outlined in the previous two sections point towards the presence of a relationship between immigration and rents in the West German housing market. The estimated effect from both OLS and IV regression are larger in magnitude then the parallel results determined in existing studies of housing markets in other countries across the globe. Possible reasons may be traced back to the specificity of the surveyed episode, which was however, a necessity for the natural experiment of German reunification to be exploited within the limited time frame of this master thesis. In addition, the related IV estimation indicates the presence of a causal migration impact on rental prices. However, the results are less concise and much larger in magnitude than their OLS counterparts, verifying the presence of attenuation bias in OLS estimates. Nevertheless, the IV estimates may also be severely biased, due to the restriction of the explored sample.

In spite of the large deviations among the strength of the suggested impact across countries, the present study lends further support to the hypothesis that immigration has a causal effect on property prices and thus the cost of living in destination economies. It further prevails, that the studies on European countries, apart from Italy, revealed larger marginal effects than the ones for traditional migrant recipient countries, such as the U.S. or Australia. Indeed, in the latter country, the estimated outcomes even showed tendencies of a negative impact of foreign born immigration.[126] Moreover, it appears that the suggested migration impact on the Swiss housing market matches the German counterpart closest in terms of magnitude. Nonetheless, a generalisation of the results across

126 See Stillman, S. and D. C. Maré (2008), p. 23.

countries and different time horizons is seemingly difficult at this stage if at all possible, since market conditions are generally characterised by local differences.

Moreover, the present analysis lends further support to the assessment of a more holistic view of the migration impact on natives. Since housing cost represent a considerably large proportion of living expenses, that is, roughly one third in the German case according to CPI data,[127] the suggested effects are crucial in the consideration of natives' welfare. This is further supported by the fact that related labour market studies surrounding the surveyed time period indicate that wages remained resilient or showed only minor tendencies of decline in response to immigration. As a result the respective scholars concluded that there was no detrimental effect of immigration on natives' employment outcomes.[128] However, taking the present study into account, immigration imposed a higher burden of living expenses to natives. Notwithstanding, an additional living cost increase may have been triggered by the migration impact on prices of other locally consumed goods and services. As afore mentioned, the study by Douglas Frank in 2007 also indicated that migration likely had a negative effect on natives, who were employed in sectors producing non-traded goods.[129] This is in line with the findings of related studies on the general price impact of migration, presented in Section 2.1. Finally, the studied data of the present investigation has shown that immigration affects rental prices of the three categories differently. Particularly, the minimum rental category was the hardest hit by rising prices due to immigration. Taken together, the discussed implications are supportive of the hypothesis that

[127] See Sachverständigenrat (2014), dataset.
[128] See Pischke, J. S. and J. Velling (1997), p. 594.
[129] See Frank, D. (2009), p. 3.

immigration had a redistributive effect from low income households to the relatively rich. This is in line with seminal studies by Albert Saiz in 2003 and others, presented in Section 2.1.

To summarise, the consideration of the housing market impact is crucial in the assessment of the immigration impact on natives. Hence, the present analysis points towards the necessity to consider factors beyond labour market effects, when it comes to formulating sound immigration policies. The development of more general models that allow a holistic view of the ways in which migration affects natives' well-being is required. Further research endeavours in this field are needed, which may include cross country analyses and adjustment for PPP. Moreover, the present study may be extended to the rural district level as well as to a consideration of whether and to what extent immigration to suburban districts exerts an upward pressure on metropolitan property prices.

5 Conclusion

The purpose of this thesis was to investigate the impact of immigration on the West German metropolitan housing market in the wake of German reunification and to explore a novel instrumentation strategy based on origin area characteristics. In order to exploit the natural experiment character of this historical episode, German district level migration data of 1991 and 1992 has been analysed in conjunction with the dynamics in West German property market indices for three different rental categories of primary let flats.

Departing from a general overview of the existing literature on the topic and a brief delineation of the historical setting that characterised the time period of interest, the empirical strategy and related data have been presented. In relation to that, the quantification of the employed data and categorisation of investigative units served to conduct a first descriptive assessment of the development in migration and property prices throughout, and prior to, the period studied. The extraordinary hike in both, German internal migration as well as property prices, provided the basis to suspect an association between the two. Accordingly, empirical evidence for the causal effect of immigration on rents in West German housing markets has been provided: A one percent population increase due to immigration is associated with an approximate increase in minimum and average rents by 4.8 and 3.3 percent. Moreover, controlling for border area location the effects become even larger, while there seems to be no indication of a significant impact on rental prices in the upper market segment. The parallel results of the IV estimation suggest stronger impacts on rental price growth, however, accompanied by larger standard errors. Namely, rental prices of minimum and average category dwellings increase by roughly eight and 4.1 percent due to a one percent population increase caused by immigration. Controlling for border area situation raises those figures to 13.2 and 7.1 percent Moreover, a significant effect for the upper market segment, worth 8.3 percent, is indicated when this special area is considered. The results are in line with most related studies; however, at a much larger magnitude, which is likely associated with the data related pitfalls of this analysis, discussed in Chapter 3 and 4.

The findings of this investigation support the proposition that immigration affects the native population of recipient areas on various grounds. Thus, the multifaceted impact beyond the sheer consideration of labour market outcomes establishes a basis for further research endeavours in this field, which constitute an essential precondition to the formulation of appropriate policy responses regarding immigration as well as housing market regulation.

Bibliography

Ahrens, Ralf (2013): *"Debt, Cooperation, and Collapse: East German Foreign Trade in the Honecker Years"*, in: Berghoff, Hartmut and Uta A. Balbier (eds.), *"The East German Economy, 1945-2010: falling behind or catching up?"* German Historical Institute, Washington, DC: Cambridge University Press: pp. 161-176.

Angrist, Joshua D. and Alan B. Krueger (2001): *"Instrumental Variables and the Search for Identification: From Supply and Demand to Natural Experiments"*, The Journal of Economic Perspectives, 15(4): pp. 69-85.

Akbari, Ather H. and Yigit Aydede (2012): *"Effects of immigration on house prices in Canada"*, Applied Economics, 44(13): pp. 1645-1658.

Akerlof, George A., Rose, Andrew K., Yellen, Janet L. and Helga Hessenius (1991): *"East Germany in from the Cold: The Economic Aftermath of Currency Union"*, Brookings Papers on Economic Activity, 1991(1): pp. 1-105.

Bodvarsson, Örn B. and Hendrik Van den Berg (2009): "*The Economics of Immigration: Theory and Policy*", Heidelberg: Springer Science & Business Media.

Borjas, George J. (1987): *"Self-Selection and the Earnings of Immigrants"*, American Economic Review, 77(4): pp. 531-553.

bulwiengesa AG, RIWIS (2014a): *"Regional Property Market Information System"*, property market data compilation, RIWIS Munich.

bulwiengesa AG, RIWIS (2014b): *"RIWIS Online - Über die Daten: Definitionen & Metainformationen"*, supplementary material, http://www.riwis.de/online_test/info.php3?cityid=&info_topic=allg.

bulwiengesa AG, RIWIS (2015): *"bulwiengesa Property Market Index 1975 - 2014"*, http://www.bulwiengesa.de/sites/default/files/propertymarketindex_2015.pdf.

Burda, Michael C. (1993): *"The determinants of East-West German migration: Some first results"*, European Economic Review, 37: pp. 452-461.

Burda, Michael C. and Jennifer Hunt (2001): *"From Reunification to Economic Integration: Productivity and the Labor Market in Eastern Germany"*, Brookings Papers on Economic Activity, 2001(2): pp. 1-92.

Cameron, A. Colin and Pravin K. Trivedi (2009): *"Microeconometrics: Methods and Applications"*, 8th Edition, New York: Cambridge University Press.

Card, David (1990): *"The Impact of the Mariel Boatlift on the Miami Labor Market"*, Industrial and Labor Relations Review, 43(2): pp. 245-257.

Card, David (2001): *"Immigrant Inflows, Native Outflows, and the Local Labor Market Impacts of Higher Immigration"*, Journal of Labor Economics, 19(1): pp. 22-64.

Card, David (2007): *"How Immigration Affects U.S. Cities"*, CReAM Discussion Paper, No. 11/07, Centre for Research and Analysis of Migration.

Carrington, William J. and Enrica Detragiache (1998): *"How Big is the Brain Drain?"* IMF Working Paper, No. 98/102, International Monetary Fund.

Cortes, Patricia (2008): *"The Effect of Low-Skilled Immigration on U.S. Prices: Evidence from CPI Data"*, Journal of Political Economy, 116(3): pp. 381-422.

Degen, Kathrin and Andreas M. Fischer (2010): *"Immigration and Swiss House Prices"*, Swiss National Bank Working Papers, No. 2010-16, Swiss National Bank, Zurich.

Frank, Douglas (2009): *"The Effect of Migration on Natives' Employment Outcomes: Evidence from the Fall of the Berlin Wall"*, INSEAD working paper series, SSRN: 1021951.

Frattini, Tommaso (2008): *"Immigration and Prices in the UK"*, Job market paper, University College London, mimeo.

Friedberg, Rachel M. and Jennifer Hunt (1995): *"The Impact of Immigrants on Host Country Wages, Employment and Growth"*, The Journal of Economic Perspectives, 9(2): pp. 23-44.

Fritz, Wolfgang (2001 [2004]): *"Statistiken der Erwerbstätigkeit in der ehemaligen DDR und ausgewählte Daten der Rückrechnung der DDR-Erwerbstätigenstatistik"*, ZA8078 datafile version 1.0.0, GESIS Köln.

GeoHack (2014): *"WikiProject: geo-referencing"*, sample URL for Aachen: http://tools.wmflabs.org/geohack/geohack.php?pagename=Aachen&language=en&params=54.781944444444_N_9.4366666666667_E_region:DE- SH_type:city%2883971%29.

German Federal Statistical Office (2000): *"Wanderungsstatistik"*, Fachserie 1/ Reihe 1.2, Wiesbaden.

German Federal Statistical Office (2014): *"Kreiswanderungsmatrix"*, annual migration datasets: 1991 and 1992, Wiesbaden.

Goebel, Jan (2011): *"Informationen zur SOEP-Geocode CD: Raumordnungsregionsnummern seit 1985 und Regionalindikatoren für Raumordnungsregionen der alten Bundesländer 1984-1994"*, The German Socio-Economic Panel Study, DIW and BBR.

Gonzalez, Libertad and Francesc Ortega (2013): *"Immigration and Housing Booms: Evidence from Spain"*, Journal of Regional Science, 53(1): pp. 37-59.

Greulich, Erica, Quigley, John M. and Steven Raphael (2004): *"The Anatomy of Rent Burdens: Immigration, Growth, and Rental Housing"*, Brookings-Wharton Papers on Urban Affairs: pp. 149–205.

Grubel, Herbert B. and Anthony D. Scott (1966): *"The international flow of human capital"*, American Economic Review, 56(1/2): pp. 268-274.

Grundmann, Siegfried (1996 [1995]): *"Die Ost-West-Wanderung in Deutschland (1989-1992)"*, in: Bertram, Hans, Hradil, Stefan and Gerhard Kleinhenz (eds.), *"Sozialer und demographischer Wandel in den neuen Bundesländern"*, KSPW-Reihe: Transformationsprozesse, 6, Opladen, Leske + Budrich: pp. 3-46.

Heiland, Frank (2004): *"Trends in East-West German Migration from 1989 to 2002"*, Demographic Research, 11(7): pp. 173-194.

Kalantaryan, Sona (2013): *"Housing Market Responses to Immigration; Evidence from Italy"*, Robert Schuman Centre for Advanced Studies Research Paper, 2013(83).

Kholodilin, Konstantin, Michelsen, Claus and Dirk Ulbricht (2014): *"Stark steigende Immobilienpreise in Deutschland – aber keine gesamtwirtschaftlich riskante Spekulationsblase"*, DIW Wochenbericht, 47: pp. 1231-1240.

Koller, Martin and Thomas Jung-Hammon (1993): *"Regionale und sektorale Schwerpunkte des Arbeitsplatzabbaus in Ostdeutschland"*, in: Mitteilungen aus der Arbeitsmarkt- und Berufsforschung, 26(1): pp. 7-27.

Lach, Saul (2007): *"Immigration and Prices"*, Journal of Political Economy, 115(4): pp. 548-587.

Ley, David and Judith Tuchener (2001): *"Immigration and Metropolitan House Prices in Canada"*, Research on immigration and integration, Housing Studies, Vol. 16 (2).

Massey, Douglas S., Arango, Joaquin, Hugo, Graeme, Kouaouci, Ali, Pellegrino, Adela and J. Edward Taylor (1993): *"Theories of International Migration: A Review and Appraisal"*, Population and Development Review, 19(3): pp. 431-466.

Meier, Christian (1986): *"Wirtschaftsbeziehungen zwischen der DDR und der UdSSR am Ende der Fünfjahresplanperiode 1981 bis 1985"*, in: Beiträge zur Konfliktforschung: psychopolitische Aspekte, 16(2): pp. 93-120.

Muller, Thomas and Thomas J. Espenshade (1985): *"The Fourth Wave: California's Newest Immigrants"*, Washington: The Urban Institute Press.

Ottaviano, Gianmarco I.P. and Giovanni Peri (2007): *"The Effects of Immigration on U.S. Wages and Rents: A General Equilibrium Approach"*, CReAM Discussion Paper, No. 13/07, Centre for Research and Analysis of Migration.

Papademetriou, Demetrios G., Sumption, Madeleine and Aaron Terrazas (2010): *"Migration and Immigrants Two years after the Financial Collapse: Where Do We Stand?"* Migration Policy Institute, Washington DC.

Perthes (1994): *"Wirtschaftsatlas neue Bundesländer: Mecklenburg-Vorpommern, Brandenburg, Berlin-Ost, Sachsen-Anhalt, Sachsen, Thüringen"*, Gotha: Justus Perthes Verlag GmbH.

Pischke, Jörn-Steffen and Johannes Velling (1997): *"Employment effects of immigration to Germany: an analysis based on local labor markets"*, Review of Economics and Statistics, 79(4): pp. 594-604.

Ravenstein, E. G. (1885): *"The Laws of Migration"*, Journal of the Statistical Society of London, 48(2): pp. 167-235.

Redding, Stephen J. and Daniel M. Sturm (2008): *"The Costs of Remoteness: Evidence from German Division and Reunification"*, American Economic Review, 98(5): pp. 1766-1797.

Roy, Andrew D. (1951): *"Some Thoughts on the Distribution of Earnings"*, Oxford Economic Papers, 3(2): pp. 135-146.

Rudolph, Helmut (1990): *"Beschäftigungsstrukturen in der DDR vor der Wende: Eine Typisierung von Kreisen und Arbeitsämtern"* in: Mitteilungen aus der Arbeitsmarkt-und Berufsforschung, 23(4): pp. 474-503.

Sachverständigenrat (1991): *"Jahresgutachten 1991/92 des Sachverständigenrates zur Begutachtung der gesamtwirtschaftlichen Entwicklung"*, Unterrichtung durch die Bundesregierung, 12(1618).

Sachverständigenrat (1993): *"Jahresgutachten 1993/94 des Sachverständigenrates zur Begutachtung der gesamtwirtschaftlichen Entwicklung"*, Unterrichtung durch die Bundesregierung, 12(6170).

Sachverständigenrat (2014): *"Verbraucherpreise in Deutschland"*, dataset available at: http://www.sachverstaendigenrat-wirtschaft.de/zr_deutschland.html#c179, accessed 20/12/2014.

Saiz, Albert (2003): *"Room in the Kitchen for the Melting Pot: Immigration and Rental Prices"*, Review of Economics and Statistics, 85(3): pp. 502-522.

Saiz, Albert (2007): *"Immigration and housing rents in American cities"*, Journal of Urban Economics, 61: pp. 345-371.

Sander, Nikola (2014): *"Internal Migration in Germany, 1995-2010: New Insights into East-West Migration and Re-urbanisation"*, Comparative Population Studies, 39(2): pp. 217-246.

Schumann, Karl F. (1996): *"Die deutsche Ost-West-Migration vor der Wende - Hintergründe und Fragestellungen eines Forschungsprojekts zur Integrationsproblematik"*, in: Schumann, Karl F. et. al, *"Private Wege der Wiedervereinigung: Die deutsche Ost- West-Migration vor der Wende"*, Weinheim, Deutscher Studien Verlag: pp. 13-65.

Smith, Lawrence B. (1974): *"A Note on the Price Adjustment Mechanism for Rental Housing"*, The American Economic Review, 64(3): pp. 478-481.

Smith, Lawrence B., Rosen, Kenneth T. and George Fallis (1988): *"Recent Developments in Economic Models of Housing Markets"*, Journal of Economic Literature, 26(1): pp. 29- 64.

Stalker, Peter (2000): *"Workers without frontiers: The impact of globalization on international migration"*, Geneva: International Labour Organisation.

Stehn, Jürgen and Holger Schmieding (1990): *"Spezialisierungsmuster und Wettbewerbsfähigkeit: eine Bestandsaufnahme des DDR-Außenhandels"*, Die Weltwirtschaft, 1: pp. 60-77.

Steiner, André (2013): *"From the Soviet Occupation Zone to the "New Eastern States": A Survey"*, in: Berghoff, Hartmut and Uta A. Balbier (eds.), *"The East German Economy, 1945-2010: falling behind or catching up?"* German Historical Institute, Washington, DC: Cambridge University Press: pp. 17-49.

Stillman, Steven and David C. Maré (2008): *"Housing Markets and Migration: Evidence from New Zealand"*, Motu Working Paper, No. 08-06, Motu Economic and Public Policy Research.

Susin, Scott (2001): *"The Impact of the Mariel Boatlift on the Miami Housing Market"*, unpublished Working Paper, U.S. Bureau of the Census, Washington DC.

Troltsch, Klaus (1993): *"Bildungs- und Erwerbsbiographien von Übersiedlern aus der ehemaligen DDR und ihre Berufsfindungs- und Qualifizierungsprobleme"*, Berichte zur beruflichen Bildung, Heft 163, Bonn: Bundesinstitut für Berufsbildung.

Wooldridge, Jeffrey M. (2010): *"Econometric Analysis of Cross Section and Panel Data"*, 2nd Edition, USA: MIT press.

Wooldridge, Jeffrey M. (2013): *"Introductory Econometrics: A Modern Approach"*, 5th International Edition, Canada: South-Western, Cengage Learning.

Annex

Table A.1: Destination Regions - West German Metropolitan Areas

Urban District	Zonal Border Region	Immigration* 1991-'92	Immigration Impact** (%)
		Schleswig-Holstein	
Flensburg	No	569	0.65
Kiel	Yes	1775	0.72
Luebeck	Yes	2521	1.17
Neumuenster	Yes	811	1.00
		Hamburg	
Hamburg	No	11121	0.67
		Lower Saxony	
Braunschweig	Yes	2895	1.12
Hanover	Yes	4431	0.86
Oldenburg	No	972	0.68
Osnabrueck	No	2112	1.29
Salzgitter	No	888	0.78
Wilhelmshaven	No	717	0.79
Wolfsburg	No	1012	0.79
		Bremen	
Bremen City	No	3924	0.71

Bremerhaven	No	918	0.70
		North Rhine-Westphalia	
Aachen	No	620	0.26
Bielefeld	No	1827	0.57
Bochum	No	1025	0.26
Bonn	No	1583	0.54
Bottrop	No	160	0.13
Dortmund	No	1662	0.28
Duisburg	No	1666	0.31
Duesseldorf	No	2032	0.35
Essen	No	1721	0.27
Gelsenkirchen	No	884	0.30
Hagen	No	939	0.44
Hamm	No	536	0.30
Herne	No	496	0.28
Cologne	No	2726	0.29
Krefeld	No	986	0.40
Leverkusen	No	594	0.37
Moenchengladbach	No	1029	0.40
Muelheim (Ruhr)	No	470	0.26
Muenster	No	886	0.34
Oberhausen	No	451	0.20

Remscheid	No	608	0.49
Solingen	No	783	0.47
Wuppertal	No	1672	0.44
		Hesse	
Darmstadt	No	784	0.56
Frankfurt (Main)	No	2860	0.44
Kassel	Yes	1744	0.90
Offenbach (Main)	No	581	0.51
Wiesbaden	No	1059	0.41
		Rhineland-Palatinate	
Kaiserslautern	No	458	0.46
Coblenz	No	481	0.44
Ludwigshafen	No	882	0.54
Mainz	No	1010	0.56
Trier	No	343	0.35
		Baden-Wuerttemberg	
Freiburg (Breisgau)	No	673	0.35
Heidelberg	No	769	0.56
Heilbronn	No	1253	1.08
Karlsruhe	No	1435	0.52
Mannheim	No	1894	0.61
Pforzheim	No	887	0.79

Stuttgart	No	5636	0.97
Ulm	No	883	0.80
		Bavaria	
Aschaffenburg	No	391	0.61
Augsburg	No	1368	0.53
Bamberg	Yes	481	0.68
Bayreuth	Yes	889	1.23
Coburg	Yes	1037	2.34
Erlangen	Yes	1077	1.05
Fuerth	No	901	0.87
Ingolstadt	No	659	0.62
Kempten (Allgaeu)	No	403	0.65
Landshut	No	273	0.46
Munich	No	9405	0.77
Nuremberg	No	4759	0.96
Passau	No	226	0.45
Regensburg	No	768	0.63
Rosenheim	No	319	0.57
Schweinfurt	Yes	261	0.48
Wuerzburg	Yes	729	0.57

Notes: * Cumulated immigration from East Germany as of 1991 & '92.
** (Immigrants/ 1990 population).

[Author's representation based on immigration data obtained from German Federal Statistical Office (2014).]

Table A.2.1: Employment Office District Composition

Employment Office District	County Level Districts *(Kreisebene)*
Berlin I-IV	Berlin (East): 11 urban districts
Brandenburg	
Cottbus	Cottbus (Urban), Cottbus, Bad Liebenwerda, Calau, Finsterwalde, Forst, Guben, Herzberg, Luckau, Luebben, Senftenberg, Spremberg
Eberswalde	Eberswalde, Angermuende, Bad Freienwalde, Bernau, Prenzlau, Schwedt, Templin
Frankfurt (Oder)	Frankfurt (Oder/Urban), Beeskow, Eisenhuettenstadt (Urban), Eisenhuettenstadt, Fuerstenwalde, Seelow, Strausberg
Neuruppin	Neuruppin, Gransee, Kyritz, Nauen, Oranienburg, Perleberg, Pritzwalk, Rathenow, Wittstock
Potsdam	Potsdam (Urban), Potsdam, Belzig, Brandenburg (Urban), Brandenburg, Jueterbog, Koenigswusterhausen, Luckenwalde, Zossen
Mecklenburg-West Pomerania	
Neubrandenburg	Neubrandenburg (Urban), Neubrandenburg, Altentreptow, Anklam, Demmin, Malchin, Neustrelitz, Pasewalk, Roebel/ Mueritz, Strasburg, Ueckermuende, Waren

Rostock	Rostock (Urban), Rostock, Bad Doberan, Buetzow, Guestrow, Ribnitz-Damgarten, Teterow
Schwerin	Schwerin (Urban), Schwerin, Gadebusch, Grevesmuehlen, Hagenow, Ludwigslust, Luebz, Parchim, Sternberg, Wismar (Urban), Wismar
Stralsund	Stralsund (Urban), Stralsund, Greifswald (Urban), Greifswald, Grimmern, Ruegen (Bergen), Wolgast
Saxony	
Annaberg	Annaberg, Aue, Marienberg, Schwarzenberg, Zschopau
Bautzen	Bautzen, Bischofswerda, Goerlitz (Urban), Goerlitz, Hoyerswerda, Kamenz, Loebau, Niesky, Weisswasser, Zittau
Chemnitz	Chemnitz (Urban), Chemnitz, Floeha, Hainichen
Dresden	Dresden (Urban), Dresden
Leipzig	Leipzig (Urban), Leipzig, Borna, Delitzsch, Eilenburg, Grimma, Wurzen
Oschatz	Oschatz, Doebeln, Torgau
Pirna	Pirna, Brand-Erbisdorf, Dippoldiswalde, Freiberg, Freital, Sebnitz
Plauen	Plauen (Urban), Plauen, Auerbach, Klingenthal, Oelsnitz, Reichenbach

Riesa	Riesa, Grossenhain, Meissen
Zwickau	Zwickau (Urban), Zwickau, Glauchau, Hohenstein-Ernstthal, Stollberg; Werdau
Saxony-Anhalt	
Dessau	Dessau (Urban), Bernburg, Koethen, Rosslau
Halberstadt	Halberstadt, Oschersleben, Quedlinburg, Wernigerode
Halle	Halle (Saale/Urban), Bitterfeld, Saalkreis
Magdeburg	Magdeburg (Urban), Burg, Genthin, Haldensleben, Schoenebeck, Stassfurt, Wanzleben, Wolmirstedt, Zerbst
Merseburg	Merseburg, Hohenmoelsen, Naumburg, Nebra, Querfurt, Weissenfels, Zeitz
Sangerhausen	Sangerhausen, Aschersleben, Eisleben, Hettstedt
Stendal	Stendal, Gardelegen, Havelberg, Kloetze, Osterburg, Salzwedel
Wittenberg	Wittenberg, Grafenhainichen, Jessen
Thuringia	
Altenburg	Altenburg, Geithain (*Saxony*), Rochlitz (*Saxony*), Schmoelln
Erfurt	Erfurt (Urban), Erfurt, Apolda, Arnstadt, Soemmerda, Weimar (Urban), Weimar

Gera	Gera (Urban), Gera, Greiz, Lobenstein, Schleiz, Zeulenroda
Gotha	Gotha (Urban), Gotha, Eisenach, Bad Langensalza, Muehlhausen
Jena	Jena (Urban), Jena, Eisenberg, Poessneck, Rudolstadt, Saalfeld, Stadtroda
Nordhausen	Nordhausen, Artern, Heiligenstadt, Sonderhausen, Worbis
Suhl	Suhl (Urban), Suhl, Bad Salzungen, Hildburghausen, Ilmenau, Meiningen, Neuhaus a. Rennweg, Schmalkaden, Sonneberg

[Adapted from Rudolph, H. (1990), pp. 487-489.]

Table A.2.2: Origin Regions - Employment Office Districts

Employment Office District	Geo Reference Centre	Border Area	Initial Working Pop.*	Area (km^2)	Emigration '91-'92**	Emigration Impact*** (%)
Berlin I-IV	Berlin (East)	Yes	721325	404	20418	2.83
			Brandenburg			
Cottbus	Cottbus	No	385687	6449	16868	4.37
Eberswalde	Eberswalde	No	176274	4842	8521	4.83
Frankfurt (Oder)	Fuerstenwalde	No	202627	4135	9762	4.82
Neuruppin	Oranienburg	No	277849	7989	25091	9.03
Potsdam	Potsdam	No	331182	5647	10712	3.23
			Mecklenburg-West Pomerania			
Neubranden-burg	Neubranden-burg	No	260766	8482	14104	5.41
Rostock	Rostock	No	294494	4541	17442	5.92
Schwerin	Schwerin	Yes	286521	7399	14010	4.89
Stralsund	Stralsund	No	191356	3416	12003	6.27
			Saxony			
Annaberg	Aue	No	200901	1593	9712	4.83
Bautzen	Bautzen	No	383626	4378	21194	5.52
Chemnitz	Chemnitz	No	297630	1002	13441	4.52
Dresden	Dresden	No	346638	583	14725	4.25

Leipzig	Leipzig	No	542575	2632	24870	4.58
Oschatz	Oschatz	No	100655	1492	4944	4.91
Pirna	Pirna	No	211517	2308	10040	4.75
Plauen	Plauen	Yes	161456	1338	6156	3.81
Riesa	Meissen	No	134218	1328	6928	5.16
Zwickau	Zwickau	No	242828	1101	9712	4.00
			Saxony-Anhalt			
Dessau	Dessau	No	157589	1398	7930	5.03
Halberstadt	Wernigerode	Yes	175895	2328	9521	5.41
Halle	Halle (Saale)	No	273963	1207	16363	5.97
Magdeburg	Magdeburg	Yes	406247	4852	18077	4.45
Merseburg	Merseburg	No	235652	2267	9072	3.85
Sangerhausen	Sangerhausen	No	141443	1849	7091	5.01
Stendal	Stendal	Yes	146483	4849	8017	5.47
Wittenberg	Wittenberg	No	87445	1695	4292	4.91
			Thuringia			
Altenburg	Altenburg	No	101979	1152	5798	5.69
Erfurt	Erfurt	No	314006	2536	14893	4.74
Gera	Gera	Yes	177927	1850	9732	5.47
Gotha	Gotha	Yes	214284	2557	10678	4.98
Jena	Jena	Yes	215952	2157	10831	5.02

Nordhausen	Nordhausen	Yes	175532	2728	8411	4.79
Suhl	Suhl	Yes	309359	3857	14273	4.61

Notes: * Refers to working population prior to reunification, precisely 30/09/1989.

** Cumulated outmigration as of 1991 & '92 from each EOD to West Germany, i.e. to the surveyed metropolitan areas and beyond.

*** (Emigrants 1991-'92)/ working population (30/09/1989).

[Data on initial EOD characteristics obtained from Rudolph, H. (1990), pp. 487-489. Emigration data obtained from German Federal Statistical Office (2014).]

MIX
Papier aus verantwortungsvollen Quellen
Paper from responsible sources
FSC® C105338

If you have any concerns about our products,
you can contact us on
ProductSafety@springernature.com

In case Publisher is established outside the EU,
the EU authorized representative is:
Springer Nature Customer Service Center GmbH
Europaplatz 3, 69115 Heidelberg, Germany

Printed by Libri Plureos GmbH
in Hamburg, Germany